D1478159

TAROT
THE WAY OF
MINDFULNESS

About This Book

Mindfulness is perhaps the most beautiful way of experiencing life more deeply.

When we work with tarot cards, all our senses are fully engaged with what we are doing. We are attentive to the present moment in which we pick and study the cards. We let the pictures affect us and explore what they mean to us currently. The cards and their motifs can open doors to deeper layers of our personality…

Included in This Book

- Tarot as a way of mindfulness
- Practical card reading
- Mindfulness exercises
- Suggestions on how to interpret each card
- Tips for your own practice

About the Authors

Evelin Bürger and Johannes Fiebig have published more than twenty tarot titles, which have been translated into thirteen languages. Their books have a total circulation of over two million copies. They have introduced and helped shape numerous standards of modern tarot interpretation, such as the "daily card" draw as a basic meditative exercise of cartomancy, the multiple meanings of each symbol, and the use of tarot cards as a psychological "mirror."

In 1989 Fiebig and Bürger founded the publishing house of Königsfurt, which later merged into the firm of Königsfurt-Urania Verlag. Today they live as freelance authors near Kiel.

TAROT

THE WAY OF MINDFULNESS

USE THE CARDS TO FIND PEACE & BALANCE

JOHANNES FIEBIG & EVELIN BÜRGER

Llewellyn Publications • Woodbury, Minnesota

FIRST ENGLISH EDITION
First Printing, 2022

Cover art by Tarot Original 1909 Deck © 2021 with art created by Pamela Colman Smith and Arthur Edward Waite. Used with permission of Lo Scarabeo.
Cover design by Shannon McKuhen
German edition © Koenigsfurt-Urania Verlag, D0-24796 Krummwisch, www.koenigsfurt-urania.com.
Tarot Original 1909 Deck © 2021 with art created by Pamela Colman Smith and Arthur Edward Waite. Used with permission of Lo Scarabeo.
Translated to English from the original German by Ilze Mueller.

Llewellyn Publications is a registered trademark of Llewellyn Worldwide Ltd.

Library of Congress Cataloging-in-Publication Data (Pending)
ISBN: 978-0-7387-6662-1

Llewellyn Worldwide Ltd. does not participate in, endorse, or have any authority or responsibility concerning private business transactions between our authors and the public.

All mail addressed to the author is forwarded but the publisher cannot, unless specifically instructed by the author, give out an address or phone number.

Any internet references contained in this work are current at publication time, but the publisher cannot guarantee that a specific location will continue to be maintained. Please refer to the publisher's website for links to authors' websites and other sources.

Llewellyn Publications
A Division of Llewellyn Worldwide Ltd.
2143 Wooddale Drive
Woodbury, MN 55125-2989
www.llewellyn.com

Printed in the United States of America

3 0646 00246 7094

Contents

Major Arcana
The Major Stages of Life

THE MAGICIAN.

THE HIGH PRIESTESS

THE EMPRESS.

THE EMPEROR.

THE HIEROPHANT

THE LOVERS.

THE CHARIOT.

STRENGTH.

THE HERMIT.

WHEEL of FORTUNE

JUSTICE .

THE HANGED MAN.

Minor Arcana

Small Steps Toward Great Goals

Mindfulness means being awake,
open acceptance of the
present moment.

Modern tarot cartomancy focuses on this attentive perception and exploration of that which is the **magic of the present moment.**

This happens primarily in three ways:

- using chance creatively in everyday life
- attentively contemplating pictorial motifs
- interpreting old and new guiding principles

Tarot and Mindfulness

Mindfulness is perhaps the most beautiful way of getting more out of life and at the same time experiencing more of one's life. Mindfulness "costs" us nothing, yet we gain a great deal by being mindful. When we are mindful, we simultaneously live life and experience it. "Awareness is conscious existence," and mindfulness is a central key to it.*

Usually, mindfulness is defined as focusing on the present moment, on experiencing the here and now. When we are mindful, we encounter all that we perceive in our interior and exterior worlds with open-mindedness and fundamental acceptance, with compassion and inner independence.

Mindfulness and Open-Mindedness

Two aspects are at the heart of mindfulness:

- expanded awareness, and
- open acceptance—perception and exploration—of what is happening.

Where Do We Start?

Modern tarot cartomancy revolves around this alert, open-minded perception of the moment. Here is how you can make a start: If you have **drawn a card** and would like to read **information** about it, you will find it from **page 23** onwards.

If you are looking for a **practical introduction to cartomancy,** start on **page 111.**

And if you would first like to deepen your understanding of **tarot as a way of mindfulness,** then begin on the **next page.**

We wish you a lot of fun with tarot!
Evelin Bürger & Johannes Fiebig

Chance Favors the Prepared Mind

Tarot cartomancy is like wakeful dreaming—meditation on images that produces a sense of invigorating relaxation. For a moment, as we read the cards, we retreat from the hurly-burly of everyday life. The "autopilot" is switched off for a moment. By the time the cards are shuffled, there's a feeling of curious and relaxed openness. Any one of seventy-eight cards may now come. If several cards are picked, we can expect an enormous number of possible combinations. This puts into perspective our assessment of our own situation and of the issues that currently preoccupy us.

If, in this spirit of mindful openness, we first simply *contemplate and examine* the cards we have picked without immediately interpreting them or drawing a conclusion far too quickly, we gain something that is important. We learn to open ourselves. As we read the cards we gain practice in what is typical about mindfulness—the "intentional focusing of attention on the present moment and on current experience."* Reading the cards prepares us for the unknown and the unexpected, and the opportunities they bring.

Mindfulness—Working Creatively with Chance

Louis Pasteur coined the groundbreaking sentence "Chance favors the prepared mind."* Since the days of this great scientist, more than a hundred years have passed. In that time, as a consequence of numerous discoveries in the fields of culture and science, chance has been considered to be a significant part of reality, ranging from important branches of physics to improvisation in art and entertainment.

One example of working creatively with chance is *serendipity*. This refers to "a chance observation of something originally unplanned that turns out to be a new and surprising discovery."* A famous example of this is Christopher Columbus, who, while he did not find his original destination of India, did find something else, something very remarkable which he had not looked for.

Serendipity refers to the kind of creative processes that enable us to discover something we did not previously look for or even know. It is a productive chance, more than simply a matter of luck, because the precondition for it is preparation, active investigation, and a certain methodology. This, too, accurately describes something we experience time and time again through reading tarot cards.

Another example that is relevant today: Greek mythology. Even the ancient Greeks knew this phenomenon, in different circumstances and by another name—chance that has significance.

Kairos—the Lucky and Right Moment

The ancient Greeks had two divinities representing time: on the one hand there was Chronos, who stood for the continuous flow of time; on the other hand was Kairos. The former represents the *quantity of time,* while the latter stands for the *quality of time.*

There are things that make us very happy when they occur. At such times, what counts is not the number of hours you spent to make things possible, but rather the fact that they happened at all. Kairos is the moment at which good solutions are possible. The reading of tarot cards is wonderful training for something else as well: for understanding the quality of time in order to see what is ripe for a solution and what is not.

Every moment, of course, is unique in a twofold sense: it is fleeting and will never return, and on the other hand (depending on the opportunity) it is of lasting significance—forever—and thus eternal. The ancient Greeks already had a phrase for this moment that becomes part of eternity: *ktema eis aei*—a possession forever.

You See the Way You See

Modern readers of tarot cards typically view the cards as a mirror. You can look into the mirror *with* other people, but not *for* other people. What do you and what do others see in the cards? What strikes you yourself in particular?

Our Own Views Count

The old-school soothsayers and practitioners of the esoteric arts assumed that every card had a fairly narrow, predetermined meaning. For instance, the Sun card was considered to be an exclusively positive card of good fortune and contentment, and the Moon was defined only in negative terms such as inconstancy, secret enemies, danger.

This began to change thanks to the Rider-Waite-Smith tarot (published in London in 1909). Pamela Colman Smith and Arthur E. Waite designed completely new images for the seventy-eight cards. That was a key prerequisite for the unparalleled tarot boom and the new, versatile interpretation of tarot (since the 1970s and 1980s). There's the saying "A picture is worth a thousand words," and now a person's own views took the place of preconceived ideas.

Pictures That Shift

The pictures of the Rider-Waite-Smith tarot especially encourage us to discover our own point of view, our personal ways of thinking. They are picture puzzles, as it were, cards with changing views.

Six of Cups: The little woman has a double face. Which one do you see first?

One of the most striking examples is the picture on the Six of Cups. It contains a double face that you often only notice at second glance. The little woman is turned away from the little man.

In one instance, the yellow is her face, surrounded on the left and right by the red and orange kerchief. In another instance, she looks at the big dwarf, and the yellow is now her braided hair, with her face to the left of it and her kerchief to the right. Usually we spontaneously notice only that she is looking in one direction, either turned toward the man or away from him. And there's a good reason for it.

This is about a return to childhood. We can—we must—set a new course (note the X in the picture suggesting switching tracks at a railroad intersection) until we are able to see both perspectives, that is, until we are free to choose between *yes* and *no* when dealing with emotional and intimate issues. Often, we initially feel something is missing; that's when we as adults need to go back to the future, take a detour into childhood, in order to gain a new inner life, a life that is now full and flourishing. This card is about flourishing spiritually, and it is the only one of the fourteen Cup cards that shows flowers in the cups.

Another example: the foot of the woman on the Star card rests on the water. In all symbolic languages (fairy tales, myths, dreams, tarot, astrology, etc.), water represents the soul, spiritual life. The foot on the water means either that the soul is supportive or that the water is frozen over, as it were, and the person no longer has access to the water world/spiritual life.

XVII—The Star: Ambivalent —the foot on the water.

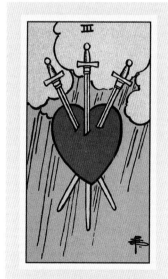

Three of Swords: The hatching may suggest a mirror or rain.

One more example: the hash marks in the picture on the Three of Swords may represent rain. This fits in with a description of this card as a card of sorrow—a scenario that is also reflected in a number of popular songs. On the other hand, such hash marks are also used to represent a mirror. This view of the image, too, is correct and appropriate. The clouds disperse and the mirror of self-awareness clearly shows us what is in our heart and on our mind, what affects us at heart.

The wide range of potential ways of viewing a picture is something we are trained to see by mindfully contemplating the image motifs. And there's more: when you see the way you see, you realize what your perspective is all about.

Experiencing Meaning and Silence

The reading of tarot cards is about the *magic of the moment*. As we saw, our experience of this magic is twofold. When we read the cards, we work creatively with chance, that is, the *moment as an element of time*. At the same time, this is about mindful perception; this is the *present moment as impartial seeing*.

A third level, a third strength of tarot, lies in the typical world of tarot images. A tarot deck consists of seventy-eight cards—twenty-two trump cards or major arcana (*arcana* being the Latin word for secrets) and fifty-six minor arcana. The latter are divided into the four suits of Wands, Cups, Swords, and Coins.

Like folktales, tarot images have developed within this structure over the centuries. And like the folktales, tarot images are a cultural heritage. The main section of this book is about this heritage and its modern-day meanings; here, each card is discussed individually.

Respond to Emotions Mindfully

Within the playful framework of reading the tarot cards, it is easier to react mindfully to emotional impressions as well. Here we can practice, even with topics we find personally shocking, not to be less attentive, but to pay more attention, so that we also learn to look at emotional and intimate issues calmly, and subsequently to act with full awareness.

A Different Way of Predicting the Future

One branch of brain research deals with *predictive coding*.* By that the scientists mean that the brain is constantly producing predictions: What's going on? Where are we? How are we? What is likely to happen? In processing ongoing sensory impressions, the brain relies on previous experiences, tries to recognize patterns, and produces these relevant predictions.

This is a very economical process. In the brain, the wheel is not being reinvented every minute, so to speak. Instead, existing patterns are applied to the current situation and modified on the basis of current sensory impressions.

On the other hand, this also means that our brain is constantly producing predictions. An additional potential disadvantage of this is that when the brain uses existing patterns, it may be less likely to optimally absorb new experiences.

In the interest of consciousness-raising, it is desirable that mindfulness should be increased and that more attention should be focused on our current perceptions. Then the odds are all the greater that we will sail through life with fresh energy rather than on the basis of outdated patterns. Thus, one objective of tarot (and of other intuitive arts as well) is to calm our streams of thought, insofar as they dwell on such perpetual inner predictions, and to create space for silence, calm, and emptiness.

"Happiness is having a talent for fate," realized the poet Novalis.* It is this talent that we develop when reading tarot cards as we interpret the major and minor arcanas. We develop it through insight and understanding as well as through mindfulness and silence.

Practicing Mindfulness I

Take some time whenever you feel like it to practice mindfulness. How frequently you do it is more important than how much time you spend doing a particular exercise. The most important thing is that you get involved. As for calm and silence, you will find them within yourself—and outside, too, behind all the sounds.

- Breathe in and out deeply. Close your eyes and feel your breath.
- Often we are obsessed with thoughts and feelings: "My neck hurts. I've got to call so-and-so. What shall I say to them? It's annoying that I haven't heard from this person yet. How do I tackle the deadline afterwards?"
- Let such thoughts come and go. Try to let them flow by you like a river. You can observe this stream, but don't do anything else at the moment. Feel your breath.
- If you notice that something is really preying on your mind, you can also postpone the meditation and first deal with the urgent matter. As soon as you're done, go on meditating. For advanced practitioners: remain in the peace and mindfulness mode even if—and especially when—you have something urgent to take care of.
- It may also be helpful to write down an important matter that you've been mulling over. That way you won't forget it and can nevertheless let go of it for the moment without worrying about it.
- Be calm and friendly to yourself. Concentrate on your breath. Let the thoughts come and go. Sense yourself, sense your body. Make a movement spontaneously and calmly and stay with it for a moment (for instance, raise your arms or put your head down, stand on one leg, pull your navel in toward the spine and up, or some other movement).

Practicing Mindfulness II

Remain mindful, even if there is a great deal in motion within you and around you.

- By means of a so-called body scan you can perceive your body mindfully. Start with your feet, the soles, and let your attention flow into every toe. Do you feel them? Now bring your attention to the arches of the feet, ankles, heels, and on from the calf and knee to the arms, fingers, neck, ears, nape, forehead, scalp, and top of the head. Can you sense yourself? What are you sensing right now?

- Initially refrain from judgment. For instance, instead of thinking, "It's bad, it really bugs me, my neck hurts," observe the pain. Where is it located? What does it feel like? How does it react if you consciously breathe into the pain? Or when you or someone else places a hand on the aching spot? What can you do with your fingers, your breath, by stretching? Ask further questions of your own as you continue exploring.

- A problem shared is a problem halved—share your experiences, ask others about theirs.

- Get help if necessary. Go see a doctor or therapist if need be.

- What feelings are you observing?

- Don't believe everything you feel! What desires, what fears seem vital to you?

- What feelings tend to represent transient emotions, ego emotions, which sometimes cloud our vision, as do some of our thoughts?

- And which feelings give you hints on what is really important now? Which emotions are like insights that heighten your perception and give you more vitality?

Ways of Mindfulness

Tarot as a Navigation System for the Soul

Tarot speaks solely through what can be seen on the cards. It shows historically stylized and symbolically condensed characters and themes from one's current life. Tarot cards are thus a special tool. They train us to recognize meanings that are also contained in everyday events, dreams, films, ideals, and many other things.

Interpret Yourself

As you start working with tarot, go through the cards and familiarize yourself with them. We also recommend you look for *favorite cards*. Conversely we suggest that advanced practitioners look for their personal *stress cards*. More about that later.

Once you are somewhat familiar with the seventy-eight cards, the excitement begins. How do you see the cards? What feelings arise at the sight of particular cards? Are there images that, try as you may, you are able to perceive only positively or only negatively? Are there themes you've never encountered in your life? Do certain images call up particular memories? Which images evoke dreams and longings?

The Daily Card

The **daily card** is basically picked (at a random point in time—the important thing is to do it more or less daily) without formulating a specific question. It represents the topic of the day for you. One stage of the tarot is emphasized as though by a magnifying glass for that particular day.

There are no mandatory rules for how the cards are to be shuffled and drawn. This holds true for all uses of the cards, whether this is a great ritual or a simple reading in-between times: Any way of reading the cards is good if it encourages you to work personally with the tarot.

The daily card—the ideal practice for novices: If you draw a card on a daily basis, you will get to know the individual tarot cards not only in theory, but directly in the context of practice, of your own experience. For advanced practitioners, the daily card continues to be one of the most important forms of practice, because this is how the interplay of changing perspectives for the individual cards and for the detail symbols becomes particularly clear. As in dream interpretation, where a recurring dream memory is usually more helpful than occasional individual dreams, in tarot too many aspects only become clear if we work on them fairly regularly.

The Quality of Time

When you draw daily cards, you get very good feedback about the quality of time. Generally speaking, the cards you draw are not regularly distributed over the days; in seventy-eight days you will probably not draw each of the seventy-eight cards once. Instead, certain motifs, certain themes will appear repeatedly and increasingly. This may induce you to explore the quality of time, the intersections and turning points in your day-to-day life.

The question novice students of the tarot usually focus on is: "Which card have I drawn?" For advanced students an additional question becomes equally important: "How do I see the card I have drawn?" Both together result in effectively, often very impressively, training tarot readers to observe the present moment.

Cards for Special Occasions

Birthdays and anniversaries. Spreads on certain anniversaries are very popular—for instance, on a birthday, on New Year's Eve, or on a day commemorating a specific event. Draw a single card (proceed the same as with the daily card) or choose a larger spread (see page 14).

Project cards or time cards such as weekly, monthly, and yearly cards: They are drawn like daily cards. Or you pull a larger spread of your own choice. Project and time cards are suitable for checking where one stands, how far one has come, and what happens next.

Project or yearly cards, in the course of their time period, frequently reveal varying visions and impressions. This heightens their appeal, for this is how, over time, varying aspects of the relevant stage of life also become much clearer.

Cards on Various Themes

The favorite card. This card is not drawn face down; it is selected with the card picture facing up. Which card/s do you think is/are best? Which card might be your favorite at the moment?

The meaning of the exercise: You pay attention to which desires are the focus of attention at any particular moment. This way of formulating questions, namely, the exploration of personal desires and fears, is one of the most important goals of mindfulness.

When our meaningful wishes are fulfilled and unnecessary fears are dispelled, we become grateful and calm. And the reverse is true as well: Calm and gratitude bring us the strength to deal with desires and passions effectively and with conscious awareness.

The stress card. This card, too, is not drawn but selected. Which card(s) do you currently reject the most? Which card would at present be your no-go?

The purpose of the exercise is more or less the same as for the favorite card. Except that the stress card is intended more for advanced tarot users who are already familiar with the cards.

The personality card. For this, you calculate the sum of the digits of your date of birth: For example, 7.9.1973 gives you 7+9+1+9+7+3 = 36. If this sum is a number between 1 and 21, then the trump card that has the same number is the personality card that corresponds to it. In most types of tarot, the trump cards may be identified by the fact that they have numbers and captions. For instance, if the sum is 19, the corresponding personality card is *XIX – The Sun*. If the calculated sum is 22, the 22 trump card—i.e., *0/XXII—The Fool*—is the relevant personality card.

If, however, as in the example above, the sum is 23 or higher, we again have to add up the digits of the calculated sum. Because the sum in the example is 36, we obtain the additional sum 3+6 = 9; the trump card with the same number is now the appropriate personality card, in this instance the number *IX – The Hermit*.

The character card. Some authors make an additional distinction between the personality card and the character card. If the sum of the digits of the date of birth is a number above 9, those digits are added up once more to obtain the character card. For example: The personality card is the number 14, whose digits give us the sum of 5, and accordingly card number *V—The Hierophant* is the character card. If the personality card has a number below 10, the personality card is also at the same time the character card.

Note: Some exercises, and particularly the personality and character cards, are an additional "game within the game." You can spend time on it, but you don't have to. You can also say: All seventy-eight cards together reflect one's own personality. The daily card(s) and an occasional larger spread on particular themes or occasions—are first and foremost the typical, important uses of the tarot.

The shadow card. For many interpreters, card number *0/XXII—The Fool* is not only an initial card, but also the 22 trump card, and thus a card of wholeness and completion. The shadow card is the difference between your personality card and the Fool. It gives you important information on the topic of personal wholeness.

If, for instance, the personality card is card number *XIV—Temperance* (No. 14), the difference from the Fool is 8 (22–14 = 8), in which case the trump card number *VIII* would be your shadow card. It denotes the shadow, the unconscious and unknown on which you need to shed light in order to fully develop your own personality.

Initially such calculations are confusing, but with a little practice and knowledge of the trump cards they will become quite easy.

Tarot Card Spreads
How to Proceed

- Make doubly sure what question you want to ask the cards.
- Shuffle as usual. Hold the pictures face down, and draw the cards one by one for the spread you have selected.

- Place the cards face down in the sequence of the pattern of the spread in front of you.
- Now uncover the cards one by one.
- All the cards combined show you the message of the tarot.

Digit Sum or Quintessence

A game within the game—not a must: At the end of a spread involving several cards, you can in each case calculate the "digit sum or quintessence." This is done using the same calculation method as for the personality card (see page 13). The digits of all uncovered cards are added together (face cards such as Queen, Knight, etc. and the Fool count as 0, aces count as 1). Once you have calculated the digit sum, you proceed as described above for the personality card. The trump card whose number corresponds to the calculated digit sum is the digit sum card or quintessence of the particular spread.

Nothing new is added by the digit sum card. The digit sum card merely represents a summary of the entire spread.

Three Card Spread

1. The current situation
2. The past, or what is already there
3. The future, or what must be newly noted

Suitable Themes and Occasions

General orientation: "Where do I come from and where am I going—what does the tarot have to tell me?"

In response to a specific question: "What path of development/solution is the tarot showing me?"

Advantages of This Spread

With this layout you can expand your daily card in an uncomplicated way if there is further need for clarification. Card 1 is then the daily card; cards 2 and 3 show the past and the future. Moreover, this spread is highly suitable for concisely assessing trends and developments.

A Look into the Future

1. Key to learning about the future or main aspect
2. The past, or what is already there
3. The future, or what must be newly noted
4. Root or basis
5. Crown, opportunity, trend

Suitable Themes and Occasions

- General orientation: "Situation and prospects—what does the tarot have to tell me?"
- In response to a specific question: "Why and how come—what happens next?"

Advantages of This Spread

Cause and effect, the situation and current opportunities take center stage here. Reserves, but also unfinished tasks from the past become apparent. So do potentials, gifts, and challenges that lead from the present into the future.

This Is Where You Go from Here

1. This is what you already know/have
2. This is what you're good at
3. This is new
4. Here's what you need to learn

Suitable Themes and Occasions

General orientation: "Where do I come from and where am I going—what does the tarot have to tell me?"

In response to a specific question: "What path of development/solution is the tarot showing me?"

Advantages of This Spread

This is a favorite spread for concisely assessing trends and developments.

The Advice of the Tarot

1. Let go of this; that's not important now
2. Learn and practice this; it will help you to move on

Suitable Themes and Occasions

- General questions on shaping one's life journey
- When one finds oneself at a crossroads
- When important decisions have to be made
- When one is searching for one's true purpose or when there are doubts about it

Advantages of This Spread

Fortunately, no one will take from you the decision of how you should live your life. You are free to make it yourself; you are the framer of your life. And if at any time you are not sure what direction this life should take you or if you doubt whether you are still on the right path, this spread can help you.

It will not relieve you of any decisions, but a look into the mirror of the cards will enable you to look at yourself and your needs. In the final analysis this is how you can check yourself in a clear and concise manner and quickly find clarity for yourself.

The Star

1. Where you stand
2. Your tasks
3. Your difficulties or reserves
4. Your strengths
5. What it boils down to/what you should do

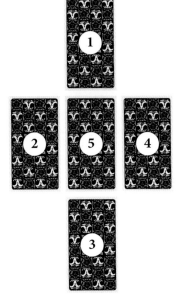

Suitable Themes and Occasions

When one wants to know the following:

- Where is this going?
- How can I zero in on a problem and bring it down to a common denominator?

Advantages of This Spread

A very exciting spread that can reveal a great deal of information to you, especially about your competencies.

The Courage to Face Shortcomings

1. That is possible
2. That is important
3. That is brave
4. That is void
5. That is necessary
6. That is bright
7. That is funny
8. That continues

Suitable Themes and Occasions
When you are stuck and have no idea what to do next.

Advantages of This Spread
With this spread you can learn a great deal, especially about the next steps you need to take.

The Path of Desires

1. Current situation
2. Desired destination
3, 4, 5. Bridge from
1 to 2

For this spread, the cards are not drawn but selected.

First, carefully choose an image for your current situation. Second, choose a card for what should be, that is, for what you really wish and aim for. Then pick three more cards that can serve as a connecting piece in order to get from what exists to the fulfillment of your desires. Finally, look at the set of cards as a path and a story.

The Celtic Cross

1. Focus of the question—you yourself
2. Positive complement to 1
3. Negative complement to 1
4. Root, base, support
5. Crown, opportunity, trend
6. The past, or what already exists
7. The future, or what should be newly noted
8. Summary of positions 1–7; your inner strength, your subconscious
9. Hopes and fears
10. Environment and outside influences; your external role
11. Summary, or a factor of which you are particularly made aware, which is already present and which will become particularly important for your question

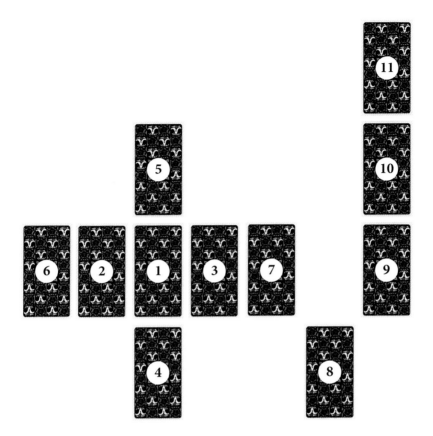

Suitable Themes and Occasions

This spread is of particular relevance for major issues and detailed answers—a true classic.

Advantages of This Spread

Here, trends, opportunities, and tasks are described in great detail. It is worth your while to take another look at the cards you drew days or weeks later and examine the practical consequences again.

Major Arcana

Major Stages of Life

The major arcana (Latin for *secrets*) invite you to engage playfully with major themes of life. Allow yourself to be touched by them and at the same time let them entertain you just as you are entertained by great films or novels. Here you will encounter **births, marriages, death**, and a **new beginning (XIX, VI, XIII, XX)** but also **heaven (XIV)** and **hell (XV)**, and possibly experiences of **loneliness (IX)**, overpowering **love (VI, XVI)**, the ups and downs of **fate (X)**, your **role in the world (XXI, I)**, and much more.

Like folktales, these twenty-two tarot images have developed over centuries. They tell us stories that are ever new, which help us to discover and tell our own stories.

Card no. *XVII—The Star*, for instance, is not only the great card of hope, it also shows lost dreams and illustrates how we may rediscover our feelings and our guiding star. *Death*—card no. XIII—is often represented as a reaper whose task it is to harvest (thus, the Waite tarot shows *Death* with a harvest crown). It reminds us to keep letting go in order to reap a harvest.

The major arcana also have daily meanings. For example, in the case of the *Star*: Fall back on your own resources. As a daily card *Death* often quite concretely means: Something is coming to an end. When something beautiful comes to an end, we mourn, and when something bad comes to an end, we are justifiably glad.

CREATIVE POWER
Making the Impossible Possible

Picture and message: Before you are the magical tools: cup, coin, wand, and sword. When you have these, the power of the four elements is at your disposal. The magic wand represents your willingness to experience yourself and your capabilities in their entire spectrum.

> *The question:* **Do you have a vision or a lifetime wish?**

I—The Magician

The challenge: Your personal magic power consists in understanding your uniqueness and in making your specific contribution. Among the numbers that are found in the tarot deck, the number One is not divisible. The Latin for *indivisible* is *individuum*.

As a unique person, you are able to perform real miracles that are ultimately normal and natural for you, while other people in their individual way create things that either do not interest you or remain unattainable for you.

What you can do: Sometimes you sense the magic that lives within you particularly intensely—when you are in love, when you are full of enthusiasm, when you are moved by the beauty of the world. You are a special person. No one can live your particular opportunities for you and no one can take them away from you! They are offered to you alone.

Going deeper: The horizontal eight (lemniscate) in the picture denotes infinity and a balance of opposites. Draw this ∞ with your left or right hand in the air in front of you several times with a sweeping gesture.

This is a way of connecting the left and right cerebral hemispheres and the sides of your body, yin and yang, heaven and earth.

ANCIENT KNOWLEDGE
& YOUR OWN SIGNIFICANCE
The Power of the Inner Voice

II—The High Priestess

Picture and message: We were once born of water, and even today we primarily consist of water. The light blue garment and the light blue water (in the background) show this existential connection. At the same time the curtain indicates separation between the self and the other.

> *The question:* **What is your most fertile source of inspiration?**

The challenge: Every person also needs "a room of one's own," as Virginia Woolf said in her essay—in real life and internally as well: as a foundation for a fruitful life of one's own. Fruitfulness is signaled by the pomegranates and palm trees in the background.

The letters B and J on the columns traditionally have various meanings. For instance, they are said to refer to *Boas* and *Jakim*, the legendary columns at the entrance to the holy of holies of the old Temple in Jerusalem. They refer to opposing forces like day and night, the polarities of life. And in the center, you see yourself. Form your own opinion and proclaim it, stand behind it.

What you can do: Sound the depth of your experiences—positive and negative, your own and others', including experiences recorded in sacred texts like the Torah. Make sense of them!—Be open-minded and mindful in your daily life.

Going deeper: Close your eyes, calm down, and imagine that you are at a place where land and water, outward and inward reality meet—and that you are receiving a special message.

ABUNDANCE & GROWTH
Drawing On Unlimited Resources

III—The Empress

Picture and message: The Empress, an embodiment of female vitality, a crown of stars on her head, sits serenely in a natural setting, close to the water. This image is about fertility, naturalness, femininity, and the feminine side of men. She is familiar with the cycles of nature and of all life, a continuous constant in her knowledge.

> *The question:* **When are you completely in your element?**

The challenge: The Empress combines a crown of stars and the earthly world, sense and sensuousness. The sign of Venus is a combination of a circle and a cross, symbols for spirit and body. The challenge lies in being present with body and soul, fulfilling the needs that are close to your heart and create momentum for new growth and new ideas.

What you can do: Being the empress yourself also means helping your own nature to bloom and flourish. Be a good wife, friend, and mother to yourself and others—incidentally, this also applies to men. This image is about the feminine and motherly sides of men, just as women also have masculine and fatherly sides. It is about nature outside in the garden, woods, and fields. At the same time the image is a symbol for your inner nature, for what comes natural to you, what suits you, and what you take for granted.

Going deeper: The pomegranate on the Empress' robe is the fruit of Aphrodite. Plant a pomegranate bush in a tub or in your garden and bond with it. Lavish care on it and enjoy watching it grow.

Authority & Self-Determination
Strengthening Life

IV—The Emperor

Picture and message: The Emperor sits on his stone throne against a blood-red sky; the ram's heads on the throne symbolize a fighting spirit. Nevertheless, sobriety and the ability to govern predominate—first and foremost, the ability to govern ourselves. Under his cardinal red imperial robe the Emperor wears his iron armor; he is forearmed at all times and is looking directly into the eyes of his vis-à-vis.

The question: **Where is there need for more consistency and assertion in your life?**

The challenge: The imperial orb and the ancient Egyptian ankh are symbols of power, but at the same time also signs of potency and fertility. This card is about structures, about power and the mission, a task which you undertake or assign to yourself.

One has to have pioneering spirit and joy of discovery, creative power and independence if one wants to "transform the wasteland into a garden" or if one wants to make a home amid the silence of stones. Be like a good husband, friend, and father to yourself and to others.

What you can do: Masculinity and power—stand up with all your might for what is important to you. Do not avoid a necessary battle; think of the steel armor under your slacks or skirt. Stand firm without giving way, and make sure you consistently develop and complete every process. Facts are acts that have been carried out.

Going deeper: Do not speak velvet words if you can perform stone deeds (*Tartar proverb*).

Teaching & Learning
The Meaning of Life

V—The Hierophant

Picture and message: The Hierophant or High Priest (formerly Pope) represents the world of faith and a deep trust arising from this faith. His right hand—the hand of awareness—is raised in a gesture of proclamation; he is a spiritual authority, instructing disciples, acolytes, or the faithful in fundamental values and virtues. Traditionally there is little room here for one's own ideas.

The question: Who imparts faith and wisdom here and now?

The challenge: At the feet of the High Priest are two crossed keys that open the gates of heaven and hell. Faith, and especially our own belief system, can become such keys for us. The High Priest embodies the teaching mind that initiates people into the mysteries of life and expects conformity. The picture may represent a challenge for you to be independent in matters of faith.

What you can do: Seek access to traditional teachings, by studying or reading. Deepen your knowledge of traditions, including those in your family, pursue some of them or create new ones. Tell others about your experiences and insights. The temple of encounters may be anywhere, including at the bus stop or on the beach.

Going deeper: Center yourself for a few minutes several times a day. This centering takes place practically spontaneously if you place both hands, palms touching, in front of your chest as is customary in Asia, or fold them as you do in church. Breathe in and out calmly as you do so or recite your own mantra or a short prayer.

DECISIONS OF THE HEART
Paradise Lost—Love Found?

VI—The Lovers

Picture and message: Many people know the story of Eve and Adam, or similar tales from other cultures. They ate of the Tree of Knowledge and were driven out from Paradise. Had it not been for this event, we would not be fallible and human in the deepest sense of the word. Love and knowledge are central themes of the picture.

The question: **What role do love and affection play in your life?**

The challenge: The angel soars above the lovers. He stands for their peak experiences and connects them with the sun. Sometimes he also resembles a gray cloud. Then he indicates trouble brewing and stress in a relationship. It is not only due to a partner that we are lovable and beautiful and unique. If we make our decisions dependent on the beloved person, it will be difficult for us to get involved in a deeper relationship and to commit to an intimate encounter.

What you can do: Open your heart without any ifs or buts! Make up your mind courageously and stick to your decision, even without a man or woman at your side. The decisions of your heart can at any time become the foundation of love, and they make you happier and stronger. To love oneself is the beginning of a lifelong romance, said Oscar Wilde.

Going deeper: People who are in love tend to forget about meditation. Similarly, people who meditate sometimes shun love. A wonderful harmony is created when love and meditation are in balance, according to mystic Osho.

THE WAY IS THE GOAL
Risking Your Own Course

VII—The Chariot

Picture and message: The chariot literally stands for experiencing one's own personality. Two components are at the center: the charioteer, i.e., the will, or conscious control, and the stone chariot, which stands for the impulses of the subconscious, for the bedrock of existence.

> *The question:* **Are you on the go? If so: Where to?**

The challenge: The charioteer in the top part of the chariot shows that you are an independent subject. The lower part of the chariot makes it clear that you have been placed within a particular life story: You cannot simply get off, though you can find the right attitude towards it!

What you can do: The sphinxes are not pulling the chariot; they are only lying in front of it. Today's riddles prepare the way for tomorrow. Solutions that are the same for everyone are one-way streets and do not lead anywhere. You will find a path of your own that is truly right for you if you walk the path of your desires. It will open before you if you ask: Which desires make sense and which do not? Which fears are justified and which are not? As long as you look for this path and apply the answers you find, everything you do is worth your while, even if it may involve hard work and detours. Conversely, even the finest achievements are worthless if they do not help you follow the path of your desires.

Going deeper: Hold on to your dreams.

GENTLE WILDNESS
Beauty and the Beast

VIII—Strength

Picture and message: Modern myths are often about a split between wildness and wisdom. The famous motif of a lion and a woman represents an alternative: Strength and gentleness, animal and spiritual strengths are joined here. Not as a circus act, but in order to tame and to appreciate the wild animal within us. Leading symbol: the lemniscate, the horizontal eight, above a head garlanded with flowers.

The question: **When do you feel your animal side?**

The challenge: The combination of enormous archaic forces and of loving strength sets something free on both sides that was hitherto submerged. This ranges from demons on the one hand to timidity or obsessiveness on the other. It takes courage and mindfulness to release and to unite both of them within us.

What you can do: The red lion and the woman clad in white denote the most powerful sides of being human: wildness and wisdom. Face wildness with unwavering gentleness and timidity with vibrant joy. Passion may play a part in all aspects of your life—in sex, at work, in sports.

Going deeper: Choose a power animal to accompany you and to give you strength for a period of time. Any animal is appropriate, from a lion to an ant, from a bee to a bear. Your power animal is an accompanying power with which you bond by way of your heart. Try for a while always to feel like this animal and see what that does for you.

THE GREAT PAUSE
Back to You

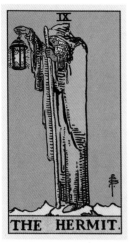

IX—The Hermit

Picture and message: The hermit in the gray cloak who holds up his lantern and leans on his walking staff signals contemplation and stillness. Here we see the archetype of the old sage who lives within us all. The snow he is standing on also symbolizes reassessment, validation, and a young, still unfamiliar terrain—internally or in the outside world.

The question: Do you love silence or shun it?

The challenge: Sometimes retreat is the only movement that will lead forward once more. Away from your daily routine and multitasking, far from demands and deadlines you can focus only on yourself and on fathoming your issues. Surrendering to the silence and stepping on the white ground covered with snow means discovering what is essential.

What you can do: Every person brings something new, something very special, into the world. Here that is represented by virgin, uncharted territory. Once we have found it, we stand on our own feet and can rely on ourselves more and more. So don't wait for solutions from the outside. Your inner light and your staff will guide and support you with all the more radiance and strength.

Going deeper: Stillness means more than do a thousand lives. It gives us a freedom that is worth more than all the kingdoms of this world. To glimpse truth within oneself, if only for a moment, is worth more than all the heavens, more than all the worlds, more than all that exists, according to poet Rumi.

ACCEPTANCE & TRANSFORMATION
The Ups and Downs of Life

X—Wheel of Fortune

Picture and message: The signs and symbols of the picture tell a special story—the same message in different languages, on different levels. Transformation and unity—both belong together, both poles form a whole and also determine your fate.

The question: How do you deal with uncertainties and shaky situations?

The challenge: We have to study many pages in the book of life, often pretty much spelling out every word, until we are able to see how things are connected. Even then life doesn't always go according to our wishes. But it is easier for us to endure hardships and perhaps even to recognize new opportunities in them. This card is about accepting fate and giving it a new twist wherever possible.

What you can do: Expect changes. The picture offers two points of reference that can give you support: The hub of the wheel is a symbol of the inner center, and of your own center and independence. The outside circle of the wheel represents experience of the universe and affection for and from other people.

Going deeper: How you deal with fate manifests itself in the way you process what "comes to you" in life. For the next ten days, pull a daily card every day. Does your day reflect these signs of the times? Write down the cards and check back at the end to see how they, as a whole, have turned up in your life.

CLEAR JUDGMENT
Weigh the Situation and Decide

XI—Justice

Picture and message: Justice raises the sword and holds the perfectly balanced scales. The dominant color of the robe and seat is dark red, the color of the *libido,* of lifeblood and love. Seemingly easily, justice holds her sword upright. It will announce the decision as soon as the scales stop moving.

> *The question:* **What was the best decision of your life?**

The challenge: Already in ancient Greece and Rome, justice was a cardinal virtue. It is not an abstract principle, but the concrete question as to how claims, resources, and wishes are to be judged and how ambiguous situations are to be resolved. How do we deal with others? How do we deal with people and matters we disapprove of? What about unfamiliar things—things we face and things within us that are unknown to us?

What you can do: Use the sword and scales to discover what certain actions mean. The more precise your investigation is, the more loving the judgment will be. Be passionate in this matter and objective in your concern. In current conflicts pay particular attention to what concerns each person involved and whether they have common interests.

Going deeper: Roughly 80 percent of your success and your good fortune is determined by about 20 percent of the decisions you make, according to the Pareto principle. Concentrate on those decisions that are really important. This applies both to the professional sphere and to private activities. Do not focus on everything and anything; focus on what is right.

PARADOXICAL BUT TRUE
Topsy-Turvy

XII—The Hanged Man

Picture and message: The hanging figure in the picture looks artistic, and perhaps kind of crazy. But there may also be some truth in the paradox. This person has a clear and unambiguous point of view, only their point of reference is not on the earth. They have a heavenly, transcendent perspective.

The question: **What is the most important turnaround you've ever achieved?**

The challenge: The Hanged Man hangs on to his faith and to his belief system. This hanging on results in a unique situation, which involves the whole person: moved by a fervor that is either a story of great suffering or an uplifting passion. In either case, do what you want if it makes you happy!

What you can do: Take your time, lots of time. Examine your belief system, then take whatever is the opposite intellectual position. Turn your world upside-down and try and figure out what it is that has been warning you for some time against going on, or what keeps you from living your truth.

Going deeper: Practice headstands or handstands or raise your legs up a wall as high as possible. Balancing on the "crown of the head" gives you a change of perspective and a new view of the world. Standing on your head promotes creative thinking, encourages blood flo, and also makes you happy.

END & BEGINNING
Death Is Part of Life

XIII—Death

Picture and message: Death approaches riding the gray horse; the persons who surround him reflect our attitude towards this. The dead king shows the ego, the child is completely open, the priest greets the rider, the young girl shyly turns away. This card is neither the concrete announcement of a death nor a bad omen. It is part of life and not the last stage in the series of the major arcana.

The question: **What in your life is coming to an end?**

The challenge: The banner of the black rider shows the alchemist's rose; with its five ears of wheat it represents a harvest crown. Without a major letting go there will be no beginning. It is in our power to check time and time again what we can harvest and where we must make room for sowing something new.

What you can do: Death is an essential part of all processes of transformation. Often it is the little deaths that we are unable to cope with. Goodbyes. Limitations. An ending. Every one of us may be dead long before we die. And you may live long after you have died—through your words and works, through the traces you leave in the world, and through the spirit that is left after you pass away.

Going deeper: Prayer Mudra* (Granthitam): Fold your hands. Breathing out and letting go become easier if your fingertips rest on the back of your hand. And the connection between human and cosmic consciousness is symbolized when the tips of the thumb and index finger touch.

WINGS OF THE SOUL
Calm and Confidence

XIV—Temperance

Picture and message: Angels symbolize our "higher self," a more comprehensive view of our situation and our prospects, an expansion of consciousness. At the same time, angels may warn us against being aloof and unworldly. Already in antiquity, temperance was one of the cardinal virtues. It has always been about striking the right balance.

The question: **What do you feel when you hear the word** *temperance?*

The challenge: Opposites that appear to be basically incompatible, like land and water at the feet of the figure in the picture, are set in motion at a higher level, analogous to the two cups. This results in creative tension, and things begin to flow again. This way, existing conflicts can be reduced to a common denominator without denying the extent of the problems. What initially seemed irreconcilable proves to be movable and solvable when viewed from a higher perspective.

What you can do: Focus on your major goals. Make sure that you are neither over- nor underchallenged. We must be at inner peace with ourselves to discover the forces that otherwise never come to light.

Going deeper: Serenity within a minute: Sit down comfortably, with your spine straight as though an invisible thread were pulling your head upward. Breathe in and silently count to four. Hold your breath and again silently count to four. Breathe out and count to four. Hold your breath and count to four. . . .

GUARDIAN OF THE THRESHOLD
Problems and Potentials

XV—The Devil

Picture and message: In tarot the Devil appears as the opposite and complement of the angel of Temperance. He is like a black box, and personifies processes that have already been subliminally present for a long time. For each of us he has a unique face. He always represents taboos—senseless taboos that are outdated and constraining, and behaviors that hurt because meaningful taboos are absent.

> *The question:* **What taboos are there in your life?**

The challenge: On the one hand, the "Devil" represents an inner tormentor that keeps making our life and that of others difficult. As soon as we are able to see the behavior mechanisms in question, we can get rid of this saboteur. He can't tolerate light. On the other hand, the "Devil" embodies a kind of neglected child. That is an important aspect of our personality which we ignore although it is part of us. As soon as we admit this to ourselves, the inner neglected child takes shape and form. It grows and develops in the light.

What you can do: Often the different sides of the Devil appear as a mix. *Diabolos* literally means *the ones that create confusion*. Separate the chaff from the wheat. At the same time, endure tensions. Don't let yourself become intimidated.

Going deeper: In order to bring light into the darkness, pull two cards. One in response to the question: "Where are there no-goes that I should ignore?" And one card in response to the question: "Which no-goes should I take heed of and reintroduce?" For two weeks, leave the two cards wherever you spend the most time.

SHOCK & LIBERATION
Plunged into Life

XVI—The Tower

Picture and message: The picture alludes to two great narratives: the Tower of Babel and Pentecost. The Tower of Babel represents human (and particularly masculine) megalomania. Its construction leads to destruction and to the "Babylonian linguistic confusion."

At Pentecost the "Holy Spirit" descends to earth in the form of tongues of fire. The Apostles begin to speak publicly, and everyone hears them in his/her mother tongue. "Babylonian linguistic confusion" on the one hand, and dissolution of language and communication boundaries on the other. Whatever the case, the picture represents special challenges when experiencing and using high energies.

> *The question:* **What within you feels like a prison?**

The challenge: The Tower warns against isolation and arrogance. New life is growing. The lightning can come from outside. It can also indicate active inner powers with the help of which one can break out of oppressive circumstances.

What you can do: Radical transformation does not happen overnight. Do not wait too long. Be present and open and do not wall in what can later turn into an explosive. Mobilize your powers.

Going deeper: Pour your heart out to somebody, one of the best ways of totally letting go. Get help if necessary. And whenever possible, offer your support to those in need. "If I knew that the world would end tomorrow, I would still plant a little apple tree today." (*Source unknown, attributed to Martin Luther.*)

YOUR SHARE OF CREATION
Tap Your Resources

XVII—The Star

Picture and message: A star of our own embodies our personal destination and confidence in a good future, which we often perceive only vaguely as a dream or longing. It appears in all innocence and is creative in a metaphorical sense. The star refers to the cosmic order and renewal at the wellsprings of life.

> *The question:* **If there is something you've always wanted to know about yourself and that no one else can tell you: What could that be?**

The challenge: The foot of the star woman stands on the water, and water represents the soul. Viewed positively, that means: The soul is supportive. In a negative case, however, there is no access to vital feelings. They seem stiff and rigid, as if frozen. The challenge consists in thawing icy feelings and getting in touch with the sources within you.

What you can do: Look within yourself. Your true self always accepts you just as you are. In the form of the two pitchers, the picture encourages us to allow our wishes and visions to flow and to see if any of them fall on fertile ground.

Going deeper: We are the miracle we've been hoping for. Your true self is creative and unique, and can look more deeply into you than anyone else. The time is now ripe to work on your personal beauty. Sometimes one has to, symbolically speaking, shed one's bearskin or hedgehog hide (as in the folktales) in order to manifest one's true nature.

TIDES OF EMOTIONS
Our Wild Soul

XVIII—The Moon

Picture and message: The stuff great cinema is made of. Great emotions. Ancient experiences (the crustacean in the picture below), strong instincts (like a dog and a wolf), and a kingdom of heaven decorated with gold (human will…). The passage between the towers, the gate of heaven, is wide open. The moon signifies a profound spiritual connection with life.

The question: **What happens to you by moonlight? What do you feel?**

The challenge: We are all part of a great stream of life, manifested as ebb and flow, an eternal coming and going. The night of a full moon can make you agitated as you perceive life's ups and downs, this world and the hereafter. In the moon, the highlights and the precipices of the soul, hopes and fears, memories, expectations, animal reflexes, and sacred promises are reflected. Thanks to your emotions, you profoundly experience joy and sorrow.

What you can do: Sense the moon within you and welcome its light. Notice your experiences and those of your family. Some moods and passions have shaped the spiritual life of generations. Descend into family myths, heroic journeys and horror stories. Much of it is unexplored territory, forgotten and repressed, and we've often been helping carry the burden of others for far too long.

Going deeper: It is precisely your emotional borderline experiences that most intensively connect you with the world and all that is human. You simply have a great soul. It is life's gift to you. Accept it!

LIGHT & WARMTH
How Lovely That You Were Born

XIX—The Sun

Picture and message: The joyous child on the gray horse is full of joie de vivre, signaled by the nodding red plume in the child's hair. A large red banner flutters in the light. Much is possible if we allow our inner child to play, radiating vitality and warmth. Sunflowers always turn towards the light—in this case towards the sun child. A little rider, but a great life.

> *The question:* **How do you feel about your inner child?**

The challenge: Having the number XIX, this card is a late station in the series of twenty-two major cards. This means that we've come so far that, now that we are grown-ups, we can become a child again. That is probably why the child in the picture has the enormous strength to carry the big banner. This card is about a vibrant and conscious existence.

What you can do: Find your center, the sun within you. In all that may come to pass, the card imparts a calm certainty, like the lovely days of your child-hood. "Just as the blossom is the harbinger of the fruit, so childhood is the promise of life," says a Sufi proverb. Whatever radiant glow reaches you from your childhood needs to be part of your life. Love and a feeling of security, but also secrets, and times when you used to be confused—give them space and light, and acknowledge them.

Going deeper: Practice a *Sun Salutation*—the well-known yoga exercise of the same name. You will easily find it in books and on the web. Or go outside and greet the sun, meditate, and feel the warmth at your center.

CALL TO LIFE
The Day of Judgment Is Today

XX—Judgement

Picture and message: We may interpret the biblical story of the Day of Judgment literally: The Day of Judgment is today! Every day anew we are called upon to wake up and accept the energies of the moment. That also means that we must really finish that which is ancient history—and open ourselves for what is coming. The rebirth that follows means new quality of life, not constant reiteration.

The question: **What miracle do you long for?**

The challenge: Take the card as a symbol for you, independent of all religious considerations: The dungeons and stifling relationships break open now, problems that have been repressed come to light, but so do wishes and hopes that haven't stood a chance so far. Resistance against changes is futile. The call has often been heard before. Now it is time to follow it.

What you can do: It is said that the angel's trumpet opens graves and awakens the dead. It is a symbol of the most powerful energies that often slumber quietly and are only aroused when there are crises and danger. But why don't we use them during good times as well? Come to life here and now with every fiber of your being and be happy and grateful for your existence.

Going deeper: When you forgive yourself and others, old tensions dissolve and new opportunities arise. Spread out your arms, as an exercise every morning or evening. Open your eyes to the colorful spectacle of life that is calling you to take part.

AT THE HEIGHT OF YOUR TIME
Your World

XXI—The World

Picture and message: You are right in the middle of the world, in the very thick of it. The two magic wands or yardsticks in the hands of the World-woman signify: Nothing can be understood solely in isolation. Anything and everything has an opposite. Decide what it is in your life that you consider essential.

> *The question:* What gifts do you give to the world?

The challenge: The corners of the picture show a traditional representation of the four basic elements fire, water, air, and earth that stand for will, soul, mind, and body. The fifth element, represented by the large figure in the center of the picture, is your personal quintessence. What is crucial is what we set in motion and how we deal with our personal world and our powers.

What you can do: Breathe life into the space you occupy in the world, experience it and shape it, and feel the sympathy the world has for you. For women, the reason why the figure of a woman appears at the center of the card "The World" is: "Recognize yourself in the world in order to understand yourself." And for men: "Recognize yourself in the woman in order to understand the world."

Going deeper: Dance whenever you would like to feel more lightness in you and bring it into the world. In the mornings, to the sound of your favorite music. Five minutes, and you will feel completely at ease and face the world with a smile. Just do it—don't think about it so much!

The Courage to Deal with Gaps
Now—Present in the Moment

0/XXII—The Fool

Picture and message: The Fool on the Cliff between the worlds, traveling light. Some commentaries say he will fall off the cliff. But in spite of everything you can recognize in the picture, the figure does not fall, and it remains completely open to what happens next (and whether, for instance, there is a meadow or a precipice below the rocky ledge). There is definitely a sage in this: What counts is the present moment and not speculations as to would happen if…

The question: **What journey into unknown territory is appropriate for you?**

The challenge: As a Fool you are free to do experiments and free to learn from them. Free not to know answers and nevertheless to trust. Don't let people make you crazy.

The zero warns against a life according to the motto "all loss and no gain." On the other hand, the zero represents a center point, a core, like the zero point of a coordinate system: the beginning and end of all that constitutes you as a person.

What you can do: "Chance favors the prepared mind," realized Louis Pasteur. The Fool carries everything he owns with him. His light bundle shows that he is able to leave his past behind him. This is what his preparation for new things consists in: getting rid of the past and opening oneself to what is coming. The zero as a circle of completing our past and as a symbol of being open to the future.

Going deeper: "Wonder is the beginning of wisdom," according to Plato.

Minor Arcana

Wands
Fire Element and Will

Something has to happen. The green shoots of the wands represent the forces in nature and in human beings that govern growth, life, and development. These shoots also symbolize a person's own instincts, urges, endeavors, and growth.

In addition to the basic human instincts—such as self-preservation and procreation—human behavior also includes love and aggression. Burning in all of us is a fire that ranges from the combustion that is part of metabolism to burning personal passions and the powerful energies of mass movements. The Wands help you find out how personal impulses and development goals work within you. Wand cards correspond to the element of fire. They are about doing something actively, or passively letting something happen and reacting to it. With Wand cards, you will find the solution you seek in action, in movement, and thus through fire energy.

Fire means the fire and energy of life, driving force and enthusiasm. In nature, it is primarily the sun, the glowing, fluid interior of the earth, all kinds of fire and lightning that emphasize the power of the element. In human behavior fire stands for will and intuition, lust for life and self-assertion, potency and creativity, commitment and power. Characteristic of the element of fire are decisions and actions. Difficult situations and trials by fire are mastered by doing something.

POWER & SELF-CONFIDENCE
Pride and Freedom

Queen of Wands

Picture and message: This queen shows how a sovereign deals with the element of fire. Her wand is that of a ruler, a woman who is aware of the effect she has and who looks out at the world full of certainty. The lions by her throne refer to power, wisdom, and wildness. This self-confident ruler stands for your courageous dominant side and also for sexual energy.

Elements: Fire and water
Symbols: Cat, lions, sunflower
Detail: The desert's changing color, transformation

The challenge: The Queen of Wands is the only queen in the tarot deck who sits on her throne with her legs apart. She is not bashful and occupies her space without hesitation. At her feet sits a black cat, a symbol of her individualism.

What you can do: Look at the flower with its stalk lopped off, in the middle of the desert. This may be a warning. The flower needs water, and besides it has no roots. Fire can easily be released, but just as easily forgets its grounding.

Yet the flower in the desert also demonstrates something else: the capacity to transform the desert into a garden! And also: to make yourself at home in the desert. The picture thus illustrates your ability to rely on your creative powers even in seemingly hopeless situations. And to create new life from an apparent void.

Feel the energy: Let the cat out of the bag! Show what you are really capable of! Bring sun into your life by living from the center of your existence. You have the ability to intervene at the right time and to set things in motion.

TRIAL BY FIRE & WILLPOWER
Responsibility and Authority

King of Wands

Picture and message: The ruler with the crown of flames sits on his throne with visible sun power that rises into the sky. The golden backrest shows the ruler's lions and the eternal cycle of life symbolized by the salamanders that bite their own tail. The King of Wands appears to be dynamic and alert. Depending on the position, this card may be a personal mirror or another person.

Elements: Fire and fire
Symbols: Salamanders, lions
Detail: King and salamander looking in the same direction

The challenge: This king is in his element; he is not resting but sitting on his throne almost as if he were about to stand up. Thanks to his spirit- and power animal, the salamander, he can walk through fire without perishing in it—as legend would have it. Like Phoenix rising from the ashes he can start all over again many times as he survives life's trials by fire and assumes responsibility.

What you can do: Accept your leadership role. You can do so privately or professionally, in sports and in the public sphere. Bravely walking through fire, combine ideals and reality. As time passes, your fire and spontaneous will are transformed into experiences, tests of courage, and tasks that gauge your strength and charisma.

Feel the energy: If you absolutely affirm ordeals by fire with this in mind, you will be all the more prepared to protect yourself against unhealthy stress.

MISSION IN LIFE & ADVENTURE
A Bundle of Energy

KNIGHT of WANDS.

Knight of Wands

Picture and message: The Knight with his charger and staff in the desert shows our ability to aim for great goals and not to let even dry spells deter us. Admittedly, like the other fire face cards, the wand with the flowering shoots in the middle of the desert also asks: Where shall the journey take you? Do you want a life in which not much is growing and thriving?

Elements: Fire and air
Symbols: Flames, salamander, chestnut horse
Detail: Flaming plumes on the helmet

The challenge: The Knight embodies a hunger for adventure and impatience, storm and stress. On the one hand, this is about the ability to aim for goals directly and to overcome obstacles. On the other hand there is the risk that there will be a lot of hot air, clouds of dust and not much more. Enthusiasm is infectious, but as you proceed you must check how productive it is.

What you can do: Do something you're burning to do. Use all your enthusiasm and motivation to go forward and to get started. Let this new beginning help you to gather momentum, and enjoy the good feeling this gives rise to. You will find solutions—and also find your inner home—by being on the move, out and about in the world.

Feel the energy: The greatest journey you can undertake—one that challenges and develops you the most—is the journey through life. Espouse worthy goals and find tasks in keeping with these goals.

Discover Your Burning Passion
All Fired Up

PAGE of WANDS.

Page/Jack of Wands

Picture and message: The Pages represent opportunities, possibilities that promise new vibrancy. In fire, the Page of Wands is in his element, and accordingly impetus that comes from him is infectious and often thrilling. The wand is taller than he is himself, and thus instinct is greater than experience, which may give it a lot of momentum.

Elements: Fire and earth
Symbols: Red plume, white hat, salamander
Detail: Flame on the hat

The challenge: Like all face cards, the Page is an image of how one of the four elements can be competently dealt with, in this case by means of the wands (the element of fire, instincts, actions, will). His youthful appearance emphasizes what is new and playful, and the urge to discover. You have drawn this card as a mirror because it reflects you, or something that is about to happen to you!

What you can do: Go for it—when you see an opportunity that excites you. That includes romance. This is not about huge actions but about the little spontaneous gestures and requests that may lead to something bigger but don't have to. Sometimes it's about a message or about being invited to take part in a new project. Recognize energies that are greater than you. Be on guard and protect yourself against narrow-mindedness. Stick to things that keep your heart beating with passion!

Feel the energy: The youthful enthusiasm that's required here is not a matter of how old one is. It's a challenge: Start something you're passionate about. Have the courage and the desire to begin something new again!

SELF-REALIZATION & CREATIVITY
The Fire Element: Urges, Actions, Will

Ace of Wands

Picture and message: Here a radiant white hand presents the wand directly to life. New strength and vitality—a tangible opportunity in our hand—suddenly grows from an apparent void. This is concentrated starting strength and action power, which has an excellent chance of success. Like every ace, this too is life's gift to you.

The number 1: Creative impulse, indivisible unity, beginning, essence
Symbols: River, fortress, trees
Detail: Eighteen green leaves

The challenge: Here we're dealing with initiative, appetite for risk and enthusiasm. Potency is in the air—after all, this wand is a phallic symbol. It is manifested equally in men and women, just as the image of the Ace of Wands applies to all genders. The new thing can be an idea, a business, an adventure, and a new life. What is most important is that you accept this creativity.

What you can do: Growth and aging seem like opposites. But both describe the same process. Aging, too, represents a kind of growth. Not just as a maturation process, but as perpetual birth: Birth is not an instantaneous event, but rather a long-term process. According to Erich Fromm, it is the goal of life to be fully born. Get ready to do this over and over again.

Mindfulness: Arrange to have a period of quiet when you will not be disturbed. Contemplate this card and think of the question. How can you best use it for yourself? What is your first impulse? What are you feeling now?

A Position of Power
The Big Picture

Two of Wands

Picture and message: Wands signify driving force, thirst for action, a need for self-realization and growth. At the same time, two wands represent polarities that block or affirm each other. Does this have something to do with a question you have asked the cards? How does one deal with contradictory lives and goals? Is the figure in the picture aware there is a second wand behind or next to it?

The number 2: Duality, yin-yang, opposites, alternatives, complement
Symbols: Globe, battlement, built by the water
Detail: Roses and lilies

The challenge: You're holding the ball. Don't get caught between a rock and a hard place. Pace yourself. Many paths lead to your destination. Wait until your view on things is finalized and until you've made your decision. Once you're ready, stop hesitating, get involved! Act with all your power.

What you can do: In order to achieve something, you must proceed step by step (wand by wand). So that you don't get stuck in the early stages and set your sights too low, the globe, a model of the whole, is so important. Hold on to that and choose with what wand, with what action you want to go on from here. That's how you will reach great goals with small steps.

Mindfulness: Affirmation: "I shall act at the right moment."

PRUDENCE
A Golden Horizon

Three of Wands

Picture and message: A traveler stands on a hill, behind him is the past, before him is a golden river on which ships are visible. The red cloak represents power. The other colors of his clothing and his relaxed posture as he holds the wand show optimism. The two wands behind him resemble a gate—a welcome for any enterprise you embark on now.

> **The number 3:** Trinity, fertility, new synthesis
> **Symbols:** Red shoes, blue sleeve or armor
> **Detail:** Sailing ships

The challenge: The right moment for proceeding will come when a decision is made from a higher perspective. The golden horizon is promising and, thanks to the stable number three, is a good basis for everything else. It is based on this foundation that the right things will happen. The fact that the gray mountain range in the distance is still before him shows that he will also have to climb unfamiliar heights.

What you can do: Work with the symbol of the golden river, longing and golden fulfillment. It is of utmost importance that you be in touch with yourself. Remain calm and be on the lookout for new opportunities. Prudence, determination, and awareness are needed here. Things will develop—don't force anything.

Mindfulness: Climb a mountain or church tower and look out at the vast landscape. While there, breathe into your belly and chest. Try to make your outbreath twice as long as your inbreath. Look forward to what is coming.

A Place of Power & High Energy
Peace and Joy

Four of Wands

Picture and message: Four bars are decorated with a large garland of flowers and fruit; they are the gateway to a celebration or a festival. Wedding? Thanksgiving? People waving with bouquets of flowers stand between the gate and the castle wall; further back there is dancing and partying. Happiness and inviting gestures welcome you. Community and joy are the signal, an invitation to be there.

The number 4: Earthly reality, four elements, new state
Symbols: Floral decorations, yellow as the dominant color, bars as the gate
Detail: Largest castle of the 78 cards

The challenge: The special composition of the picture clearly emphasizes the welcoming, festive mood and joy. It is a happy "open house" at a place of power where the energies increase exponentially. A safe place where people can open up and enjoy being together. That is difficult for many of us, for we have become lone warriors and are not easily able to open up.

What you can do: Feel you are welcome; there's a good reason why the gate is lavishly decorated. Walk toward the others and say hello to them. Consider in what situations you find that hard to do. This card is to be filled with life when it is drawn. If that doesn't happen, the topic of being welcome is still emotionally charged and unresolved.

Mindfulness: Disrupting routines and taking a different route than usual produces mindfulness. Dance at the next party (if you usually never dance), eat with your left hand (if you usually eat with the right hand), and shake hands when you say goodbye (if you usually just wave) or wave (if you usually shake hands).

FRICTION & DECISION-MAKING
Competition and Cooperation

Five of Wands

Picture and message: Five young men playfully fight with their staffs. They are all in motion; it's a competition and a testing of skills. They all have the same chances; none have advantages or disadvantages. These contests are the basis for teamwork and partnerships, as well as a suggestion that one should accept fiery energy and closeness and let oneself in for comparisons and trials of strength.

The number 5: Quintessence, five senses
Symbols: Cloudless sky, youth, sprouting wands
Detail: Different-colored shoes

The challenge: When there are skirmishes and competitive behaviors, there is friction. It is important that different motivations, interests and attitudes be allowed to struggle and compete with each other. The basic conditions for this are only being created now, and this is still fighting without rules. The signal: Don't be afraid of competition!

What you can do: Open yourself to the play of forces within you, with you, and around you.

Allow yourself to be touched by people, energies, and events. Join the game and feel the energy. As you do so, you can learn to exchange blows creatively—as in Aikido—and to utilize the energies of others by accepting, parrying, and at best even transforming them.

Mindfulness: Feel what is going on inside you when there are confrontations or frictions. Do you judge the other person(s)? Are you sympathetic, hostile, or annoyed?

Learn nonviolent communication.

BE AN ACTIVE PARTICIPANT
Together You Are Strong

Six of Wands

Picture and message: In the center we see a rider who towers above all the other figures in the picture. He rides a white horse wearing a green caparison, and is accompanied by several persons who have five more wands. We can hardly make out some of these companions except by the wands they carry. The rider has a green wreath on his head and on his wand.

The number 6: Past, present and future, penetration
Symbols: White horse, red and green cloak, two wreaths
Detail: The gaze of the horse

The challenge: You develop your optimum power when you empathize with all the figures in the picture and thus come to understand the different roles, and when you account for your strengths and weaknesses in all your actions. Act, and don't hide your light under a bushel.

What you can do: Often we think we have to suppress weaknesses in order to have pride and strength. The picture shows that the reality may be different. Those who care for strengths and weaknesses gain additional powers, as manifested here in the horse and in the energy of the five wand bearers (next to the large figure of the rider). These represent influences and events that are out of our hands. However, if you engage and involve these forces, you will expand your ability to "cooperate with fate."

Mindfulness: Show what you're capable of, and do not hide even your weaknesses. If you follow something for which you have a weakness, it too will support and take you forward. Repeat the affirmation: "Together I am stronger."

A Burst of Energy & Leap Forward
Assertiveness

Seven of Wands

Picture and message: The picture appears to show a man alone against the rest of the world. He's being attacked or feels attacked, though he is on firm ground and able to fight steadfastly and skillfully. He repels the six wands, very determined to defend and hold his position. The message: Show your skills offensively and not let yourself be impressed by superior strength or pressure.

The number 7: Seven days, years, wonders of the world
Symbols: Green hill, gray precipice, cloudless sky
Detail: Different boots

The challenge: Fighting spirit and readiness to engage in conflict are now required. One's own standpoint (both literally and figuratively speaking) must be firmly defended. Self-assertion, including against a superior number of adversaries, is a challenge when an equivocal stand must be taken. This is where one needs to make a smart chess move or take a bold step.

What you can do: Defend your territory and put up a vigorous fight—including against rivals or groups. Even when you encounter envy or jealousy, or when people try to undermine you, stand up and make your position perfectly clear. Fight for yourself and what you are and have achieved.

Mindfulness: Look at your body: Your spine is upright. For two minutes, focus on a body part of your choice. What does it feel like? Move this body part in different directions. How does that feel? Which muscles work to make this movement possible?

INCREASING RANGE OF INFLUENCE
What's Up?

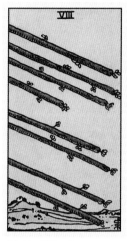

Eight of Wands

Picture and message: This picture is puzzling, for it involves eight flying wands that will land somewhere or that have just lifted off. They are underway. The sky is clear, the green landscape is hilly and gentle, a river meanders through the countryside. The only thing that suggests people is the house on the hill, There's definitely something in the air. News is on the way, possibly with a surprise in store.

The number 8: Upright infinity symbol, cyclical change
Symbols: Miniature world, wands like arrows
Detail: Deserted landscape

The challenge: What kind of news is coming is not clear yet. It's still in the air, in parallel formation. It will be something good—fresh, fiery impulses and favorable developments. From experience we tend to believe that there will be trouble when something unfamiliar approaches. But this is about trust, openness, and flexibility.

What you can do: Get inwardly ready for changes. Look into what moves you and what you set in motion! You can be noncommittal, for the impulses come from outside. Once they are there, be open and ready for anything. Be happy about a new vibrancy on many levels. This is all-important: It will come sooner than you think.

Mindfulness: When stressed or expecting something new, we often react too quickly and too rashly. Use a pause for breath to react more consciously, mindfully and deliberately: Breathe deeply into your belly and breathe out again very slowly before you react to an event.

STEP FORWARD & SHOW YOURSELF
Mindful Perception

Nine of Wands

Picture and message: Wands symbolize fire and instincts. The lush green of the landscape shows growth and maturation. The varying lengths of the wands point to different kinds of developments.

Does the person in the picture know what is happening behind his back? Is he aware what is going on?

The number 9: Abundance, complexity
Symbols: Fence, gap, bandage, headband, stalking
Detail: Ambiguous facial expression

The challenge: The headband possibly refers to wounds suffered by the figure. But maybe the figure also represents a huntswoman stalking or a scout on the path: attentively looking in all directions, wide awake. Sometimes it is impossible to see the forest for the trees. Or one knows nothing about the many happenings behind one's back. What prevails at times like this are routine and overcautiousness. Holding back, so to speak. And we miss the greater mystery that is waiting for us "out there."

What you can do: Look with both eyes, listen with both ears, inwardly and outwardly. With intuition and by staying alert you will also succeed in leaving certain fears behind you.

Mindfulness: Everyone has strengths and weaknesses. Often we concentrate on the weaknesses and thus reinforce them all the more. Write down in detail now what three of your great strengths are. And recall them every day upon waking.

STRENGTH & CONCENTRATION
Let a Hundred Flowers Bloom

Ten of Wands

Picture and message: The picture shows a man leaning into his bundle of wood who holds on to the wands to keep from scattering them in all directions. This person is totally dedicated to his task, carrying his cross with all available energies and a strong sense of purpose. This may lead to great success, or he may wearily pack it all in; the outcome is uncertain.

The number 10: High point, conclusion and reorientation
Symbols: Border line, red tunic
Detail: Personal inclination (posture as a symbol)

The challenge: The man does what must be done, only he doesn't do it particularly skillfully. Bundles of wands are hard to carry this way; it would be easier if they were tied and shouldered. This card is about lots of responsibility, possibly too much of it. The result is overwork, and a solution should be found quickly. Exploitation and self-exploitation must be prevented at all costs.

What you can do: If you feel you have taken on too much, then shed some ballast and consider what your life is really about. Do your goals make sense? If not, drop everything else that burdens you and let go of everything. If they do, put your heart into what you are doing, be focused, and prepare for your great success.

Mindfulness: For three minutes, turn your awareness to the way you walk. Feel how your feet tread on the ground. Sense how your heels, the balls of your feet, and the tips of your toes unroll. Turn your awareness to your breath and bring the rhythm of your footsteps into harmony with it.

Cups
Water Element and Soul

The container that gives form to water. Cups are traditionally assigned to the element of water. A characteristic of water is its fluid, amorphous state; on the other hand, a characteristic of the cup is its fixed form. Water is not tangible; it is cups that make it possible to collect and handle it. If water symbolizes our feelings, then cups represent everything that gives our feelings a receptacle, form, and shape: psychological and spiritual needs of all kinds, faith and longing, our inner life in every concrete form.

Cup cards represent opportunities to be in the flow, to allow something to flow, or to receive something. They are about sympathies and antipathies, about feelings—lovely and bad and all the rest—about joy and sorrow, emptiness and fulfillment.

Water is the elixir of life, covers the greater part of the Earth's surface, and is the main component of the human body. It connects all life. In nature, the moon, rain, and bodies of water of all kinds express the power of this element. In human behavior, its power is primarily expressed by thirst, tears, drunkenness or sobriety, emotion, empathy, moods, and premonitions. Characteristics of the element of water are receptivity, compassion, and devotion.

The Preciousness of the Soul
Near Water

QUEEN OF CUPS.

Queen of Cups

Picture and message: This queen sits as if draped on her shell throne; she and her gown practically flow toward the water. The covered cup, decorated with angels, and the shell-shaped backrest of the throne express wealth, protection, and openness of the soul. The Queen of Cups, as custodian of the water kingdom, shows her feelings and her creativity, moved by the tides.

Elements: Water and water
Symbols: Shells, mermaids, throne on sand
Detail: Red shell brooch and red lining of the cloak

The challenge: Now is the time to stand by your feelings and to respect your inner voice. No other tarot figure embodies the preciousness of spiritual life as clearly as this one. Your task is to be a source of inspiration, like a fairy or enchantress, and likewise to approach the dark side of the soul.

What you can do: Live a deep and fulfilled daily life. Set psychic boundaries and also open yourself in order to constantly renew and purify your inner source of water. This way you will be in flow and at peace with yourself and the world, and can summon up strength and productive imagination. You have a knack for relationships, spiritual talent, and seasoned wisdom, which can thaw frozen-over souls, as it were.

Feel the energy: Open your heart to a male or female friend, listen to a suffering or loving person, and sympathize with their situation. Look inward and let images and intuitive feelings arise.

MASTER OF FEELINGS
Heart Thoughts

King of Cups

Picture and message: The King of Cups is the king of the heart. His task is to account for all his great feelings, to give them space and at the same time never to lose sight of his contact to his source. His intuitive knowledge and his leadership are shown by the open chalice and his scepter. The open sea behind him is much frequented. He sits on the throne and rules with distance and strength—himself and others as well.

Elements: Water and fire
Symbols: Flying fish, blue garment, chainmail shoes
Detail: Wears a fish pendant

The challenge: The water world with all its depths is the kingdom. Does it support us? The fish and water snake suggest feelings that are usually hidden below the surface, while wishes and fears float to the top. Consciously dealing with emotions and passions makes for inner momentum and points the way—slow, steady, with the innermost truth always present. The king's yellow cloak indicates sunny warmth.

What you can do: You are a loving, dignified person who draws great strength from the depth. Your inner life and feelings are of great importance for you. Draw on unlimited resources and build dykes that will protect and limit you. Always make sure you have detachment from your rich world of emotion so that you will not get lost in it. Show compassion and help those who are weaker.

Feel the energy: Go for a walk alone by a river, a lake, or the ocean. Look beyond the horizon. Explore the wordless knowledge in you and listen to the silence.

TRUTH OF THE SOUL
Lived Faith

Knight of Cups

Picture and message: The knight sits erect on his white horse, on the way to his spiritual truth and the goals of his heart. The cup in his hand attests to that. He is in the flow and inspired by his thoughts and feelings. His armor shimmers like water. This card is about affairs of the heart at every level of human existence.

Elements: Water and air
Symbols: Wings on helmet and spurs, open visor
Detail: Red fishes on the surcoat

The challenge: Great feelings and passions, lifelong dreams, and important personal goals are always also a matter of faith. Peacefulness and sincerity are manifested in this knight; the cup in his hand indicates he is facing an invisible someone or a spiritual goal. The task is to be willing to embrace peace and love and to reach out to others—easier said than done.

What you can do: Examine your core beliefs; they are your armor, and they envelop and accompany you. Let your loving and peaceable side precede you with the cup, and follow it with your entire being. If your glasses make the world look too rose-colored, then take them off and trust in your wonderful warm-heartedness.

Feel the energy: Spend one day giving happiness. Bring joy to others and enjoy their joy. Declare your love if you are in love, and let your heart speak when words are too much.

LIGHTNESS OF HEART
Floating Free

Page/Jack of Cups

Picture and message: Pages like this one are the grist of our mill. They are a romantic impulse, a loving offer. The gently smiling boy stands on a sunny ground, the moving water behind him. His goblet is filled with a real fish; he himself stands in a graceful posture, as if he were handing the goblet to someone. It can be an invitation, an offer, reconciliation or an advance.

Elements: Water and earth
Symbols: Light blue headgear, scarf "spills" over
Detail: Pale pink water lilies on the shirt

The challenge: The Page wears his "heart on his sleeve," the cup is raised, the fish, which is usually in the water and below its surface, is clearly visible. Loving feelings are being offered, and the question is what the response to them will be.

The flowers on the figure's tunic represent the fruitfulness of inner life.

What you can do: Remain lighthearted. Don't be afraid of being committed to your feelings, of being passionate, of daydreaming and remaining open. By empathizing with others and searching for deep insights you will come to experience your spiritual and emotional abundance more and more. Find the Holy Grail within you and look into it more deeply. Don't play games with the feelings.

Feel the energy: Send out loving impulses and be open to the response. Go to a body of water and listen to the sound of lapping waves; watch the fish and listen to Schubert's *Trout Quintet*.

THE HOLY GRAIL
The Water Element: Soul, Feelings, Faith

Ace of Cups

Picture and message: A radiant white hand offers the golden chalice to the world. Above it soars a white dove that holds a host marked with a cross above the chalice. Five fountains spout water into the waterlily pond, accompanied by little drops of water. This is an offer and an opportunity to comprehend your own chalice—the vessel of the soul—anew, and to allow this wellspring to overflow.

The number 1: Creative impulse, indivisible unity, start, essence
Symbols: Dove, cross, waterlilies
Detail: Bells on the stem of the cup

The challenge: The picture alludes to baptism, the spiritual rebirth from water and spirit. In the chalice is life-giving water, which, connected with the whole and at the same time elevated on your hand, is your own innermost grail. The task: To plunge into the great stream of time and experience being connected with the universe.

What you can do: When you succeed in establishing a personal balance between yourself and the world at large, you will experience a wonderful fountain of youth. Let your feelings bubble up, overflow, and take you to a new level. Use this unique gift to go with the flow of life, and to be connected with what's above and below, inside and outside.

Mindfulness: Every morning in the shower listen to the splashing of the water, pay attention to the sound of the drops on your body, watch the water forming beads on your skin, and shower gel bubbles bursting. In your mind, stay close to the water.

WINGSPAN OF THE SOUL
Attraction and Bonding

Two of Cups

Picture and message: Two people face each other; they hand the cup to each other. Above them, the magical symbol of the two serpents entwined around the staff of Hermes, is a symbol in alchemy for the joining of opposing forces and of sexual attraction. The winged lion's head symbolizes power and protection. This polarity may give rise to love at first sight, a loving encounter and also a contract.

The number 2: Duality, yin-yang, opposites, alternatives, complement
Symbols: Two cups, poppy wreath (his), laurel wreath (hers)
Detail: The lady wears red shoes

The challenge: Two cups emphasize the polarities of our inner life—sympathy and antipathy, affection and dislike. Everyone has to discover for themselves and reflect on the famous "two souls housed in [their] breast" (Faust). This card is also about partnering with someone, giving something and receiving something. This may be love or some other kind of partnership.

What you can do: If you encounter love, be in the flow and enjoy the encounter wholeheartedly. Sometimes what seems wonderful at first glance, namely, the sharing and exchange of the cups, is difficult. It depends on your expectations and also on your longings. If you are looking for a "better half," you will be disappointed until the balance between your wishes and feelings improves.

Mindfulness: Look at your beloved or another person who is dear to you as though you saw them for the first time—their facial expressions, gestures, the way they talk, their body. Take it all in and sense your own emotions as you do so.

THE MAGIC OF THE SOUL
Treasury of Experience

Three of Cups

Picture and message: Life becomes a joyous festival when there is gratitude about growth and fertility. The sumptuous fruit on the dance floor and the luscious cluster of grapes in the hand of the woman on the right show the harvest. Old traditions are involved: triple goddesses, the three Graces (Grace, Beauty, Joyfulness), the three Norns (Fate, What Is Presently Coming into Being and What Shall Be), the three magic wishes in the fairy tale …

The number 3: Trinity, fruitfulness, synthesis
Symbols: Wreaths of flowers, harvest, cloudless sky
Detail: Raised cups

The challenge: All good things come in threes. Many consider this card one of the most beautiful in the tarot deck. Something essential has been achieved, an important phase has been concluded. Joie de vivre and fulfilment find glorious expression here. The way the three women hold their cups represents not only grace but also their pride. Interesting: Depending on the viewers' life situation, the group of women has a different effect on them.

What you can do: Gather the fruits of your labor and of your successes and celebrate them wholeheartedly. Enjoy this time with friends, dance and laugh and have fun together. Be grateful for your rich harvest and look forward to your next period of creativity and success.

Mindfulness: The necessary precondition for peace and a joyful existence is realizing that peace and joy are possible, according to Buddhist teacher Thich Nhat Hanh.

One's Own Roots
Retreat and Inspiration

Four of Cups

Picture and message: The tree is a symbol of nature, and also a symbol of human growth and becoming. Since the figure in the picture sits by the roots of the tree, this means he is outside in nature, and symbolically near his personal roots, his origins, regardless of where he is living at the moment.

The number 4: Earthly reality, four
   elements, new status
Symbols: Red sweater and red shoes,
   tree, green hill
Detail: Cup from the cloud

The challenge: Meditate—or take care of whatever prevents you from meditating and being still. In silence you will find names and words for experiences and tasks for which you have hitherto had no language. Let your soul go limp. And sum up your feelings and spiritual experiences in a new way.

What you can do: A new experience awaits you, a hitherto unprecedented offer. You can accept this new cup. Or you can reject it, as in "Let this cup pass from me!"

For one, you need to interrupt your everyday routine and calm down. For another, you need to stop brooding, get up and stretch your arms to the sky.

Mindfulness: *Wu wei*, action in inaction: Lie down or sit down. Deliberately do nothing in the next three minutes. Pay attention to nothing, look at nothing, think of nothing. Get a sense of what doing nothing feels like.

A TIME OF TRANSFORMATION
Past but Not Over

Five of Cups

Picture and message: A tall dark figure stands in a landscape with a castle or ruin and a river and bridge. Three cups have been knocked over; two cups are ready to drink from. The sky is gray—colorless, indistinct or else undecided, neutral.

The number 5: Quintessence, five senses
Symbols: Bridge, castle, yellow shoes
Detail: Red wine (lifeblood)

The challenge: You encounter unfamiliar feelings. Don't run away from them! Perhaps you are mourning something that is lost. It takes time to understand what it really is. Perhaps this is about a disappointment. It offers an opportunity to say goodbye to illusions and to make a new start into new clarity. Tears are all right, but also new perspectives and new enthusiasm if you are ready for it.

What you can do: The soul functions like an inner mirror. It is precisely those things of which it has no image it can reflect as yet that appear dark to the soul. Initially the soul has only a dim notion of all that is really new to it!

What feels like a spiritual blackout may also be a side effect of a real change in your personal life circumstances. Then walk down the "tunnel" unafraid and look forward to what is coming.

Mindfulness: Deliberately leave room for sadness and grief. With dignity, release what can't or doesn't want to be with you any longer. Open your heart and your arms, say goodbye and feel that space is being created for something new.

BACK TO THE FUTURE
Flowers for the Soul

Six of Cups

Picture and message: The fairy-tale world adorned with flowers is reminiscent of a time when wishes still came true. Six cups filled with white flowers, a homelike place that promises protection. One cup is up on the pedestal, another is in the hand of the big dwarf. This encounter gives us a glimpse of something old to which you now need to pay attention.

The number 6: Past, present and future, penetration
Symbols: White flowers, optical illusion, the watchman or wanderer
Detail: White gloves

The challenge: The picture contains a now-famous double face. The little woman is looking away from the big dwarf (the yellow is her face, framed by the red-orange headscarf). Or she is looking his way (the yellow is now her braid, with her face to the left of it and the headscarf to the right). Mostly we spontaneously notice only one of these perspectives. Our perspective on experiences from our childhood is similarly split.

What you can do: Deal gently with your emotional experiences. Try to recognize the true version—that is, your lived reality. Ask yourself how you can bring back the lovely experiences of former times, and how you can keep the bad things that happened once from recurring today. Here and now, you have sustainable alternatives for handling wishes and fears, and can find different solutions today.

Mindfulness: Opening oneself to pain and at the same time being your own witness is the way of mindfulness. An effective approach is to be with yourself with close attention, to feel the difficult feelings—as you play the part of the friendly observer. This friendly presence creates space for good things to happen within it.

Wishful Thinking & Truth
Searching Your Soul

Seven of Cups

Picture and message: A shadowy figure contemplates seven cups on a big gray cloud. Fantastic possibilities open up here. Or is that a mirage? Examine your emotions. Is there a cup whose contents particularly attract you?

The number 7: Seven days, years, wonders of the world
Symbols: Shadowy figure, cloud, no earth
Detail: Hands protrude under the white cloth

The challenge: The head symbolizes beauty, but also vanity. The tower-like fortress stands for power and greatness, or alternatively for isolation. Pearls and jewels speak for themselves. The next cup has a laurel wreath, for death or victory. The dragon represents the forces of the underworld that may devour you, or else bring good fortune. The serpent is known both for its wisdom and for its falsehood and base motives. The seventh cup, finally, is a mystery; it stands for new miracles or yet unused psychic forces.

What you can do: Scrutinize the needs and personal goals you have at the moment! Sometimes the greatest longing and the most unrealistic desire represent exactly what is right for you. Or the smallest temptation and the most harmless promise may end in tears and pain. Seek clarity.

Mindfulnes: Gift yourself a gentle smile. If you like, close your eyes as you do so. This will help you recollect the smile more easily. It can be quite faint, so that it may be barely noticeable outwardly.

DEPARTURE & SEARCH
Follow the Flow

Eight of Cups

Picture and message: It is dark. The moon moves in front of the sun, and watches the wanderer from the sky. He sets out on his journey with a heavy or joyous heart. Until now the cups have been clearly in the foreground; now he sets out for a future that is still uncertain. The red boots and the red apparel tell us that he is leaving of his own free will. Whatever is old is out of date.

The number 8: Upright infinity symbol, cyclical change
Symbols: Yellow walking staff, red boots, sun and moon
Detail: Vast river landscape

The challenge: In tarot, cups are always about the inner life. Here, the forces of the soul are in motion. Our soul needs this, just as plants need fresh water. When we journey to the source, we return to the roots. If we walk toward the estuary, we follow our destiny. The river connects the source and the estuary. If we stay with it, we are always at home and on our way!

What you can do: You cannot step into the same river twice, says Heraclitus. Everything is changing and in a state of flux. Sometimes the inner river is in danger of drying up; sometimes it threatens to flood the landscape. Trust your inner stream and your flow. With the power of your soul you will give form to what is formless and find your way.

Mindfulness: Walk as if you were kissing the earth with your feet, says Thich Nhat Hanh. Simply set out and focus your eyes on the ground two meters ahead of you, and you will stay with yourself. As your feet rise and fall in your tempo, you can focus your whole attention on the sensations in them.

Great Soul
A Multitude of Feelings

Nine of Cups

Picture and message: This card is about all kinds of cups—feeling, insight and faith, the whole broad spectrum. Almost the entire range of emotions comes into the picture, and the man with the wide smile in front of his cups sits there and is very satisfied, perhaps even too self-satisfied. The row of cups is behind him, a little above him.

The number 9: Abundance, complexity
Symbols: Sunny space, reddish-yellow socks, blue curtain
Detail: Wooden bench

The challenge: The man is obviously presenting his collection of cups to the viewer. Yet he distances himself, with his arms crossed and red turban. To live and work with a lot of emotion and with a great soul is a precious gift. It is pure happiness, though sometimes we don't realize it or think we don't deserve it. What could be in the cups?

What you can do: The figure in the picture has to turn around in order to see the nine cups. When one dissociates from feelings and traumas, they sometimes lead a life of their own. Adopt the posture of the man on the card. Legs apart, smiling, arms crossed. Feel all your cups and your wealth, and sense how your soul expands and your whole being resonates to this.

Mindfulness: Take several deep breaths in and out. Be grateful. Recollect your day. Forgive yourself and others for yesterday's mistakes. Smile at yourself. Welcome what is about to come.

HARMONIOUS PASSIONS
Trusting Yourself

Ten of Cups

Picture and message: The rainbow as a bridge between heaven and earth, filled and fulfilled by ten golden cups, signals: Everything is good! This calls for joy! A deep emotional bond.

Attention: The cups in the rainbow may also represent emotions that are divorced from reality, and hermetical belief systems, like a glass dome!

The number 10: High point, conclusion and reorientation
Symbols: Rainbow, home, glorious colors
Detail: People in motion

The challenge: In many cultures the rainbow is a symbol that is filled with light. Sun and rain make this phenomenon possible, and it often signals pure joy. The rainbow stands for the land of dreams "over the rainbow," and also for the good fortune at the end of the rainbow. It is a symbol of creativity, of the creation of all kinds of opposites. Look forward to shaping your life as a multifaceted work of art.

What you can do: In emotional and spiritual life, too, there are pros and cons. You can tell the difference between clear and troubled water. The rainbow appears after a cleansing thunderstorm. Being happy is a transient state and does not last forever. Savor your happiness without trying to hold on to it, enjoy what is, and take pleasure in the intimacy of the moment.

Mindfulness: "We already have all the things we require to be happy. We must simply allow ourselves to live in the present moment to get in touch with them," said Thich Nhat Hanh.

Swords
Air Element and Mind

The weapons of the mind. Thinking, knowing, judging. Sword symbolism goes back, among other things, to the ancient image of Justitia, whom we encounter on card no. XI of the major arcana. This goddess of justice—one of the four ancient cardinal virtues—has always been depicted with a sword and scales. This sword was not only an instrument of power used to enforce a judgment, but, like the scales, also a tool for forming judgments: Scales are for weighing things, and a sword is for examining and distinguishing things. With a sword, you can make cuts and make dividing lines, revealing what belongs together and what does not.

Sword cards correspond to the element air. They are about penetrating and illuminating something mentally or about being permeated and inspired by air and spirit. Air means the atmosphere of the earth, breath, vital spirits, mental energies, and worlds of ideas. In nature it is primarily wind, air, air space, and the stars—which only twinkle for us thanks to the layers of air that surround the earth—that demonstrate the power of the element air. In human behavior it is presence of mind and the power of ideas, conceptualization and formation of conscience, communication, and performance arts. Characteristic of the element air are insights and decisions. Difficult situations are overcome by mastering the necessary learning curves.

GIVING STRUCTURE TO FREEDOM
Independent and Smart

Queen of Swords

Picture and message: The queen is a strict judge and a funny elven queen. The crown is made of fine metal, but at the same time it is a dance of butterflies. The left half of the figure's face is hidden. References to her other sides are provided by the head of the child, crescent moon, and butterfly on the gray throne. She is alone and stands for independence and clarity, solves problems with her mind and wisdom.

Elements: Air and water
Symbols: Butterflies, double ax/crescent moon, angel or child's head, cloud dress
Detail: Ribbon on the arm

The challenge: This ruler makes intelligent decisions. Like all face cards this image shows the queen competently dealing with one of the four elements, here with swords (the element air, insights, concepts, judgments, intellect). The card emphasizes your feminine side. You are getting this card as a mirror, because this is what you are like or because you can be like this!

What you can do: The strength to learn new things and the independence to work only on projects you can stand behind on all levels are your true luxury. Nobody tells you what you should or should not do. Use your qualities as you make smart and unconventional decisions. Be blunt, say what you think, and clearly and firmly support what needs to be done.

Feel the energy: Today, solve an urgent problem, make a conscious decision, and look beyond would-be practical constraints. Be careful in your evaluations and insightful in your judgments. Paint your favorite butterfly.

Understanding What You Love
Doing the Right Thing

King of Swords

Picture and message: This king looks at us directly. He holds his sword in his bare hand. His is the world of ideas and of the intellect, in which he shines. His butterfly and crescent moon throne rises into the sky, and is placed in a fertile landscape. With his intelligence, he is able to unite heaven and earth—a ruler who is a solver of problems.

Elements: Air and fire
Symbols: Butterflies, sky blue robe and gray-violet-red cloak
Detail: Couple on the throne's backrest

The challenge: This card is about an intelligent king who is able to help others. This type of analytical mind may belong to a consultant, a therapist or a lawyer. Wide awake and focused, he keeps a cool head even when emotions and difficult decisions are involved.

What you can do: Pay attention to the birds (here and in the pictures of all four Swords face cards). From a bird's-eye perspective, you can have a clear view of basic needs and pending tasks. The two birds (in contrast to the bird of the Queen of Swords) symbolize highflying ideas and do not stand for spiritual needs only. They may also refer to sexuality, something birds have symbolized since the Middle Ages. You have great visions and passions. Cultivate them!

Feel the energy: Look for intellectual challenges, join debates, and play chess. Observe birds. Solve complex puzzles and compile decision-making techniques. Dealing respectfully with love and passion will make you both great and light; it will truly give you wings.

INSIGHT & PASSION
Intellectual Confrontation

Knight of Swords

Picture and message: The Knight of Swords spurs his horse, dashes forward with his sword raised, in full armor, his visor still raised. Clanking metal from head to toe, red plumes fluttering in a tempestuous ride—here icy confrontation is in the air, at best a decision and clarification of important matters.

Elements: Air and air
Symbols: Red flowing cloak, speed
Detail: Birds and butterflies on the bridle

The challenge: A tempestuous ride of ideas. Breakneck intellectual pace and radicality. Clear consequences are required. Solutions that promote the integrity and satisfaction of those involved. Don't let anyone stop you.

"For when you love something that is hardly within your reach,
that seems unattainably far away, you become a bit sad.
You become a dreamer. Or you become a radical.
Or a radical who makes his dreams come true."
—*Susanne Zühlke*

What you can do: Stop thinking inside a box and don't hide. It's up to you to clarify and affirm the path you are taking. Often it is crystal clear words and signals at the right time that lead to becoming powerfully effective.

Feel the energy: "Once someone has recognized his situation, how could he be stopped?" asks Bertolt Brecht.

BREATHING SPACE
A Fresh Breeze

PAGE of SWORDS.

Page/Jack of Swords

Picture and message: The page stands on a hill, ready for action—supporting leg and free leg, the sword in both hands. Clouds are billowing and the trees sway in the wind. Pages bring offers— here, there is a struggle for clarification so as to create breathing space and drive away the clouds. His youthful appearance emphasizes what is new and playful and speaks of an urge to explore the world.

Elements: Air and earth
Symbols: Red boots, hair blowing in the wind
Detail: Flock of birds above the clouds

The challenge: Keep the sword in your hand. Don't hand over your power of judgment to others. A flame in the fire, a body in the water, or an object in the air gets a boost from a gust of air. In a figurative sense, this is also true of the human mind, to which the air element is symbolically assigned. The true test of a functioning mind is that it makes many things easier.

What you can do: Focus on new ideas and have patience. Protect yourself from arguments that are made up out of thin air. Protect yourself from credulity and cluelessness. The sword in the backhand shows indecisive or devious behavior.

Feel the energy: Perhaps you feel that the part human beings can understand is smaller than what exists. It makes a big difference whether you understand and make use of the part that is yours, so that life for you and your fellow human beings becomes easier, more conscious and more entertaining. Pay particular attention to this today, and try it out!

THE CORONATION
The Air Element: Insights, Concepts, Judgments

Ace of Swords

Picture and message: A sword in the clouds and high above them: a symbol of enlightenment, human consciousness as the crown of creation. The epitome of nature (note the branches on the sword). Warning against the destructive force of the mind. Know that it is your gift and challenge to grasp and understand the sword—the weapon of the mind—in a new way.

The number 1: Creative impulse, indivisible unity, start, essence
Symbols: Branches (or branch and algae), six golden drops
Detail: Bare mountains

The challenge: Swords are two-edged—an elementary challenge for us all. Yet the spirit that permeates everything also creates unity. It is the special role of the Ace of Swords card to use the sword in an enlightening and clarifying way as you resolve and eradicate problems. Get to the point. Identify a common denominator. Refine, analyze, and keep an eye on the big picture.

What you can do: Now is the time to deal with your creative power mindfully. Pay attention to what is and not to what was or what could be. Your mind will unfold to the full when it frees itself from its conditioning and expands to embrace the absolute, the unconditional—and when it makes itself practically useful. Sharpen your awareness, that's what counts now. Remain calm, even in in shaky situations. Be clear when others obfuscate, curb your emotions, this is not the place for them.

Mindfulness: See that your thoughts correspond with your actions. Free yourself from doubts and ambiguities. Fortify yourself with what you know, and bear in mind what you do not know.

Comprehending the Invisible
Spiritual Vision

Two of Swords

Picture and message: A blindfolded female figure sits on a stone bench, her back to the water, with two swords crossed in front of her chest. She holds the swords, the weapons of the mind, and points them far beyond herself. The ocean of emotions and instincts is close by. Appearances can be deceptive—what is happening behind her back?

The number 2: Duality, yin-yang, opposites, alternatives, complement
Symbols: Gray clothing, rocks in the ocean, moon
Detail: What looks like a third eye

The challenge: The blindfold is a sign of impartiality. Here it serves clarification, and promotes relaxation and inner distance. It is good for fantasy and imagination. Sometimes it also points to a lack of perspective, when your inner self is trying to tell you something—something you should be aware of and understand. Beyond appearances begins the realm of the spirit. It is in this realm that your current questions can be found.

What you can do: Just as a wireless operator establishes contact with distant continents, it is now important for you to come to know and understand areas of your life and your psyche that extend far beyond your direct range of experience. From the visible parts of the rocks in the water you can extrapolate that there are invisible parts under the surface of the water.

Mindfulness: Jin Shin Jyutsu for relief: Holding a single finger with the other hand brings improvement. The thumb regulates worries, the index finger reduces fear, the middle finger dissolves rage, the ring finger comforts, the pinky brakes zeal.

Insights & the Knowledge of the Heart
Head and Heart

Three of Swords

Picture and message: This card has often been understood as the "card of sorrow." Yet it also means something else, just as, for instance, the hatching in the picture indicates not only rain but also a mirror. Three swords pierce the heart. This may be an image of pain, of being hurt and of torment. Or something quite personal for which there can only be an individual response.

The number 3: Trinity, fertility, new synthesis
Symbols: Heart, rain, mirror
Detail: No blood

The challenge: Neutrally viewed, the picture shows an interface: The weapons of the mind pierce the heart. Two different systems—the conscious and the subconscious, mind and heart, external arguments, and inner experience—are connected by this interface. You are offered the opportunity and the great challenge to understand what is close to your heart and runs in the blood.

What you can do: Many problems are due to the separation of the heart and mind. This is what leads to fixed ideas; they can paralyze large areas of the mind, and like a thorn in the flesh they cause constant pain. Speak openly—do not conceal what is in your heart.

End old sorrow without creating new sorrow. Recognize what deeply moves your heart or the hearts of other people.

Mindfulness: According to an Indian proverb, it takes just as long to grieve about the past as it does to shape the future.

Peace of Mind
A Good Conscience?

Four of Swords

Picture and message: The figure in the picture lies on the bed as though turned to stone. A sword below it, three swords above it. A scene of spiritual weariness and numbness, or else of concentrated intellectual activity. The word PAX, peace, appears in the halo of the figure giving a blessing in the mosaic window.

The number 4: Earthly reality, four elements, new condition
Symbols: Mosaic window, jigsaw puzzle, pillow
Detail: PAX

The challenge: Seek peace and find clarity. Perhaps you have done and experienced a lot that you now need to vent. Or you are about to face important events. Many impressions need to be processed until a mosaic, a complete picture and a suitable plan can be created from many tiny particles. With a clear plan and a good conscience you will feel light and fully alive.

What you can do: Meditate and switch off the movie in your head. Don't get stuck in virtual worlds! "Thinking is one of the greatest pleasures of the human race," said Bertolt Brecht. See to it that you have insight and understanding for real events, real problems and experiences of real happiness.

Mindfulness: A calm mind is an active mind. It is like relaxed breathing—it wants to be left alone to do its work. In order to flow calmly, it would like to solve existing problems that might create a logjam. Help your mind to do this. Meditate. Finish whatever is outstanding now.

GROWING AWARENESS
Learning from Experience

Five of Swords

Picture and message: Three figures stand at different distances by a river or lake; they differ in size, and partly turn their backs to each other. The smallest figure holds his hands before his face. The biggest carries three swords, while two swords lie on the ground. The three figures may represent different persons, but may also be three aspects or stages and developmental phases in one person's life.

The number 5: Quintessence, five senses

Symbols: Redheaded man in red clothing, swords on the ground

Detail: 3 figures as aspects of you

The challenge: Don't switch off when there are difficulties, but mobilize your mental powers. Notice the two swords on the ground: They warn against improvident thoughts, unutilized intellectual gifts, which can become stumbling blocks. Doubts you have overcome and shed are a reason to be pleased.

What you can do: Learn from experience, your own and that of others. Make peace with various phases of your life. The times when you felt infinitesimally small are behind you (speaking from the perspective of the figure in the foreground of the picture). Today you are much further along than you were then. Looking back today, you can understand and eliminate previous difficulties. Learn to make allowances for weaknesses.

Mindfulness: "You must be the first to forgive, smile and take the first step. Don't wait for others to forgive, for when you forgive you become a master over fate. You shape your life. You perform miracles. Forgiveness is the highest and most beautiful form of love," said Serge Kahili King.

TRANSITION
In Touch with the Origins

Six of Swords

Picture and message: Traditionally the figures in the picture are interpreted as a ferryman, woman and child. The ferryman punts the boat with a black pole. There are six swords in the bow of the boat. The swords—the "weapons of the mind"— act as a compass or navigation device. Or they represent old ballast that is being transferred to a new situation. The card is also about an intellectual transfer, a mental relocation and new decisions.

The number 6: Past, present and future, penetration
Symbols: Black pole, light blue horizon
Detail: 3 figures as aspects of you

The challenge: Ferrying from one bank to the other is a step into the unknown. That is hard. Usually it is associated with insecurity and anxiety; many mental swords have come along on the journey. Interests and new facts need to be clarified. It is important to find help or to be of help to another person who is in quest of new shores. The new territory may be professional, private, regional and family-related.

What you can do: Trying new things despite anxieties is part of life. Proceed cautiously and deliberately. Figure out what your interests and needs are. Your disputes should literally be in-depth. Use your mental flexibility and the intensity of the moment to find out what needs actually move you and other people. Make sure others know what your needs are!

Mindfulness: Let your intelligence be like the pole in the picture: an aid you can rely on because you have contact to the origins. Try to understand what others basically mean by what they do and say.

Puzzle and Solution
Eliminating a Dilemma

Seven of Swords

Picture and message: Going forward and looking back: a symbol of inner strife and unresolved conflicts. Or a picture of conscious confidence in one's own journey, a picture of self-assurance: "Life must be lived forwards, but it can only be understood backwards," says Sören Kierkegaard.

The number 7: Seven days, years, wonders of the world
Symbols: Camp, yellow sky, ochre-colored earth
Detail: Cloud on the horizon

The challenge: Each of us brings along our own truth into the world, and as long as we are separated from this truth that is specifically our own, we are searching! That's how we encounter personal mysteries that we initially barely notice and then at first can't understand.

We should remain mindful, but not ignore aggravations and vulnerabilities. They help us to search and find new solutions.

What you can do: Good fortune on your journey through life depends on how you define yourself in relation to others. Understand what bothers you and others. Draw distinctions and set yourself off from others without ceasing to feel concern for them. Be deliberate in your actions. "If you do not apply what you have learned in what you do, you end up no longer being able to tell what must be done," says Horst-Eberhard Richter. Emphasize every step.

Mindfulness: A Buddhist maxim advises to walk when you walk. See when you see. Hear when you hear. Feel what you are.

GRASPING THE INCONCEIVABLE
Consciously Controlling One's Behavior

Eight of Swords

Picture and message: Often we primarily see captivity or diffidence in this picture. If that is so, the picture also says: The swords make it possible to sever ties that hinder us. Seen from another perspective, the card represents a life that is consistently navigated by mind and consciousness. Often the card also represents contemplation and a questioning of inner knowledge.

The number 8: Upright infinity symbol, cyclical change
Symbols: Bonds, blindfold, red robe
Detail: Fortress in the background

The challenge: The blindfold warns against lack of perspective. On the other hand, it stands for impartiality. The cords around the arms and body warn against inability to take action and against powerlessness. Yet a spiritually conscious life only begins beyond appearances and beyond that which is concrete and comprehensible! This is what the current questions are about.

The fact that the head and arms, or rather the torso, is bound here also means that thinking and action are connected. Thus this card challenges us to be particularly consistent and to behave with especial commitment.

What you can do: Examine your beliefs. Inappropriate beliefs hamper us, while appropriate ones liberate and strengthen us even as we allow ourselves to be "fettered" by them!

Mindfulness: "There are ideas you cannot understand unless you change your life," said Werner Sprenger.

New Insights
Spiritual Work, Inner Maturing

Nine of Swords

Picture and message: It's gotten dark. Or else light penetrates the darkness. Nine swords symbolize ideas and insights which are interlocked. They may be the reason why the figure in the picture literally looks at the dark side and covers its face with its hands. If we look at it another way, the figure covers its eyes in order to get used to the light that the swords— the "weapons of the mind"—cast into the darkness as flashes of inspiration and new insights.

The number 9: Abundance, complexity
Symbols: A web of swords, roses of insight
Detail: Scene on the bed

The challenge: We keep pushing forward into unexplored and unexamined spheres of life. That can be scary, particularly when an entire spiritual horizon, a network of ideas appears in a new light. What is involved here is the expansion of consciousness, the discovery and exploration of new spheres.

What you can do: In your thinking, advance further than ever before. Get used to new perspectives and connections. There are leaps forward when you abruptly realize the consequence of something you've already been practicing for a long time. Don't be afraid! Give yourself time and space to process the new insights.

Mindfulness: A basic exercise frequently used in training the eyes is palming. Palming means lightly placing the balls of your thumbs on your cheekbones with your palms cupping the eyes. This is how your eyes relax.

End of the Performance
Fruits of the Mind

Ten of Swords

Picture and message: It's getting dark. Or a new day is dawning. A figure is lying on the ground, with ten swords in its back. Viewed neutrally, the picture shows that our concepts, assessments and judgments, the weapons of the mind, "nail us down" to real consequences. This situation very much depends on the meaning of the "swords"!

The number 10: High point, conclusion and reorientation
Symbols: Dusk or dawn
Detail: Finger position like that of the Hierophant

The challenge: Here, from varying perspectives, we see the fruits of the mind. The negative version: You would rather hold on to impractical, fruitless ideas, even when they are ruining you. The positive variant: The seed of good insights germinates and produces a rich harvest. You don't have to be a guru, philosopher or other type of mastermind to have an abundant intellect. Are you ready to act with deliberation and awareness and to go beyond models and habits?

What you can do: Be open to a fundamental change of mind. In the face cards of the swords we keep encountering butterflies. In the sword cards with high numbers we come across the process of transformation from a caterpillar to a butterfly: In the Eight of Swords the caterpillar spins itself a cocoon. Nine swords show the process of maturation in seclusion, while the ten swords show a leap into a new existence.

Mindfulness: It is what it is, says love. *Erich Fried*

Coins

Earth Element and Body

Coins, or the face of the earth. *Coins* is the traditional term for this suit. Sometimes they are also called discs, pentacles or stars. We human beings are like the coin. On the one hand, we are shaped by circumstances; on the other we shape our circumstances ourselves. The tarot of A. E. Waite & P. C. Smith emphasizes this idea by showing a pentagram in the Coin cards; among other things, this is a code, a symbol for a human being. Like a minted coin, every person has outstanding and less outstanding characteristics, gifts and handicaps. The experiences and insights resulting from these shape our personal differences; they are our talents.

In other words, coins represent talents, material and personal values, something shaped and the forces that shape it. It is generally accepted that they correspond to the "element earth." Earth means matter, material, physical life—the material circumstances of human lives. This means our bodies and the earth on which, and thanks to which, we live. In human behavior the forces of the element earth are primarily expressed in practical skills and talents, in sensual perceptions and physical sensations as well as in practical tasks and material achievements. Characteristic of the element earth are products. Difficult situations are mastered by creating a stable form for something: It's the results that count.

TALENT & GROWTH
Fruitfulness and Dedication

QUEEN of PENTACLES

Queen of Coins

Picture and message: The Queen of Coins, ruler over the Earth, sits in a lush landscape on a throne adorned with an angel's head and fruit ornaments, ibex and steer. Her crown is decorated with cherries and angels' wings; her flowing green veil signals rich growth. In her lap she cradles the golden coin as though it was a child she plans to protect. The cycle of nature is the miracle she serves.

Elements: Earth and water
Symbols: Climbing roses, blue mountains, hare
Detail: Wings and jewels on the crown

The challenge: This card is about being close to nature and the cycles of life. The roses hang from black vines; they symbolize the eternal cycle of growth and decay. The little hare is a symbol of fertility. What is called for is a sense of reality and family values, dependability, and a talent for giving optimum support to the natural world. Meanwhile, keep in mind the feasibility principle.

What you can do: Bank on pragmatism and business acumen, far from all pipe dreams and castles in the air. Proper grounding, as well as a feel for material processes and cycles are called for here. Use your creativity and sensuality, and your sixth sense, for the right path or the right project. If you have a family, you will be the warmhearted and caring mother and partner that is modeled by this queen.

Feel the energy: Work in the garden, plant something, walk through the botanical garden, recycle, bake a cake, have a meal with your family or friends.

Sensuality & Pleasure
Joy in Life and Work

KING of PENTACLES.

King of Coins

Picture and message: A contented king sits here, his crown adorned with red flowers, his robe opulently ornamented with grapes and golden leaves. A total of four steers signal abundance and security, sensuality, and equanimity. The secure fortress behind him indicates stability. Contentedly he holds the coin, he enjoys his life. But his foot, shod in knight's armor, shows he is ready to do great deeds.

Elements: Earth and fire
Symbols: Grapes, scepter, steer heads
Detail: Grapevine

The challenge: This is about your work and your achievements. The grapes symbolize the enjoyment of life—both sensuous and sensual, physical and spiritual enjoyment—"there is truth in wine!" Winegrowing is the epitome of strenuous, patient work. Joy in the result and the enjoyment of the fruit of the vine are the reward for the proverbial work in the vineyard.

What you can do: "It is folly to pray to the gods for that which you have the power to obtain by yourself," says Epicurus. You are an epicure, a planner and organizer who through his work finds peace in life. Prove yourself and develop as the architect and builder of your life. Stop doing annoying chores—or transform them into work you can enjoy. Construct a work of art from your various tasks and achievements—your life's work.

Feel the energy: Enjoy a good wine or grape juice. Be aware of what you have achieved, and share your joy with friends and companions.

Sowing & Harvest
Persevering and Prudent

KNIGHT ᴏꜰ PENTACLES.

Knight of Coins

Picture and message: The Knight of Coins sits on his black horse looking out over the tilled fields. He protects the fields from sowing to harvest—the treasure that is also mirrored in the coin. Oak leaves, a symbol for steadfastness, adorn his helmet and the horse's bridle. He is a watchman who can be relied on, his horse stands still, and he too is at repose. To be in his company means to be secure.

Elements: Earth and air
Symbols: Armor, open visor, red glove
Detail: Oak leaves on the helmet

The challenge: The function of the Knight of Coins is to create values with diligence, perseverance and tenacity. His observation skills and equanimity are in demand now. The horse's fiery red tack and the knight's surcoat of the same color attest that both of them can get started at any time when it is essential and appropriate.

What you can do: What do you want to harvest? Start looking for ways to implement your ideas. Patiently, step by step, you will get closer to your goals. A pragmatic approach is the basis for solid results. This is a good time to implement all the feasible and valuable ideas that have been floating around in your head and vanishing up till now. Look out for tangible results.

Feel the energy: Make something by hand, such as pottery, painting or baking. Or do something physical like riding, jogging or gymnastics. Collect change in a piggybank.

FIND OUT WHERE YOUR TALENTS LIE
Inquiring Minds

PAGE of PENTACLES

Page/Jack of Coins

Picture and message: The pages represent opportunities that present themselves along the way, promising new vitality. The Page of Coins carefully balances the coin, which indicates his talents, on his fingertips. A golden sky illuminates the scene. The young man knows what he wants; his red head covering shows self-confidence and willpower, while his brown boots show his down-to-earth attitude.

Elements: Earth and earth
Symbols: Green tunic, grove of trees, farmland
Detail: Coin and sky appear to be one

The challenge: The Page of Coins is an excellent guide who can lead you out of the holding pattern of "would have, could have, might have" to a place of realistic implementation. This is where gifts and talents and the daily magic of making and acting can be used. We often think our own talents are insignificant because we take them for granted. Actually, however, all of us have valuable talents that we need to discover, embrace and implement during our lifetime. Now is your chance to do that.

What you can do: Gear yourself up for new practical opportunities and use them. The coin is life's gift, your value, which you can experience more and more by opening yourself to the tangible suggestions and offers that are now coming toward you. You should not pass up a good opportunity to earn money. From now on, distinguish promises from offers and get actively involved.

Feel the energy: Go out into the countryside, look at the fertile fields or blooming meadows, keep your eyes open, be prepared to get going at short notice.

Value Added
The Earth Element: Body, Talents, Finances

Ace of Coins

Picture and message: From a cloud, a radiant white hand holds out the coin. The gifts of life and of the earth appear below it invitingly, in blossoming abundance. For many the Ace of Coins is the luckiest card of the minor arcana, and this luck is waiting to be discovered. Every ace brings a gift of creation through which we experience life's abundance. Here it's our sense of reality, our understanding for the tangible things in life.

The number 1: Creative impulse, indivisible unity, start, essence
Symbols: White narcissi, gateway into the world
Detail: Coin with double edge

The challenge: The double edge of the coin points to the double nature of us humans: born of matter and spirit. Coin cards all show a pentagram, a code for a human being; the corners of the five-pointed star represent the head, hands and feet. The Ace of Coins is about shaping matter and about creating exactly the life we wish for. This gift can now be used, in the best possible and luckiest way.

What you can do: Think big! Take pleasure in being acknowledged, in money and in delightful developments. This is not the card of sober austerity, but of self-realization and success. See yourself and your life as a gift, and thank Creation for the wonders of your world. You are one of those wonders, and it is vital to live this wonder with all your senses and talents.

Mindfulness: Every night, find five things you are grateful for. These may range from a parking spot in front of the door to the kiss of a friend, rain after days of drought, or professional success. Focus on those things and take the feeling with you into the night.

Changing Values
Finding Balance

Two of Coins

Picture and message: The figure in the picture demonstrates the art of working with "both sides of the medal." The Two of Coins represents past and future, the sun and shadow sides, things compulsory and optional, general norms and your personal life rules as well as many other contradictions. The green ribbon of the horizontal eight that surrounds the coins points to vitality, becoming and growing.

The number 2: Polarity, yin-yang, opposites, alternatives, complement
Symbols: Tall red hat and red leggings, sailing ships
Detail: Stormy sea

The challenge: Every new transformation is associated with a reassessment. The figure's striking hat points to a possible temporary imbalance in your consciousness. Eyes and ears, all your senses may currently go haywire for a while. Your perceptions are shifting and expanding. Emphases are changing. You may experience ups and downs.

What you can do: You need a good center of gravity within you, the right ballast and skillful steering, as illustrated by the two ships in the picture. You need good balance, a clear mind with free-floating attentiveness and no inner clinging.

Mindfulness: With arms outstretched join both palms together in front of your chest at heart level. Draw a large horizontal eight, in a sweeping loop toward the left, switch to a loop toward the right. The crossing point is always at your chest level. Follow the movement with your eyes while your head and body remain upright.

PROGRESS & VOCATION
Latent Talents

Three of Coins

Picture and message: Three people stand in a vault contributing their skills and views to a project: a stonemason, at work on a bench with a mallet, as well as a monk and a fool. The three coins with the pentacle symbol are black—only here—and part of a building. This is not about mere work and income, but about the broader context of professional development and devotion to a project.

The number 3: Trinity, fertility, new synthesis
Symbols: Blueprint, workbench, fool
Detail: Black coins

The challenge: Here your personal qualifications are demonstrated—under the keen eyes of experts. Professional, spiritual and personal progress is made visible and checked for validity and reliability. Skill and maturity are put to the test and applied at a higher level than before as you work with others. The transparent coins show the spiritual background of a great work.

What you can do: It makes a considerable difference whether you reach the peak of your gifts or not. Perfect a current project that brings out your best energies. Voluntarily face tests in order to manifest your gifts and to continue mastering the skills you have. This will affect your self-confidence, change you and take you to new spiritual realms.

Mindfulness: "Why do you believe that work and meditation are two different things?" asked Akong Tulku Rinpoche.

Taking Possession of Oneself
Can't Be Too Sure

Four of Coins

Picture and message: A man sits with the tips of his toes touching two large gold coins and hugs another one to his chest with his arms and hands. He is holding it in front of his heart chakra, while the fourth coin sits directly on his crown. Every person has talents of their own: special gifts and specific limitations that ground them, that are close to their heart, and that crown them.

The number 4: Earthly reality, four elements, a new situation
Symbols: Oversized coins underfoot, city at one's back
Detail: Crown as a coin holder

The challenge: Don't play the hero or the loser. "All of you is worth something, if only you will own it," says Sheldon B. Kopp. The most valuable talents are those that provide the most benefit. They are especially beneficial when they meet as many human needs and relieve as much distress as possible. It is vital to put your own talent to use now.

What you can do: Only play it safe if it is unavoidable. Check whether your risk management is up to date and make clearly defined agreements. The city is far away in back of you. Sometimes it is important to deliberately distance oneself in order to focus attention on one's own intrinsic value, or discover it in the first place and to try it out. Sometimes, however, it is also important to confide in people more and not to turn one's back on others.

Mindfulness: Affirmation: "I now stop trying to force things and gratefully accept what life has in store for me."

DISTRESS RELIEF & COMPASSION
Necessities

Five of Coins

Picture and message: On a winter's night two people pass by a brightly lit church window, completely locked into their misery. They do not see the golden coins in the window; both are sick and the winter is cold. This is a crisis with all the risks it entails, and life is fragile. There seems to be no help for these two—perhaps they're not looking for it either, but keep on walking aimlessly.

The number 5: Quintessence, five senses
Symbols: Church window, crutches, cold
Detail: Plague bell around neck

The challenge: When there is poverty, suffering and hardship, the feeling of being excluded spreads, and we believe we are helpless and without hope in times of trouble. But there is help even when times are tough; the brightly lit window is a radiant guidepost—to people, values and institutions that are ready to help, and to those who are standing right next to you.

What you can do: Human capability is valuable, particularly when it helps relieve severe hardship and gives new hope. If people around you need help, use your talents to contribute to their welfare. If you yourself are in trouble, pause for a moment and ask for help. Don't wait for a miracle, but go where you can receive tangible support.

Mindfulness: A legend tells of the blind man and the lame man who set off together. The blind man supports the lame man and the lame man guides the blind man. As they share their problems and talents, they are no longer daunted by the helplessness of their situation.

GIVE & TAKE
Benefit for All?

Six of Coins

Picture and message: In the left hand of the large picture figure we see a scale; with the right hand it hands out coins to the kneeling beggars. There is a balanced relationship between give and take; the balance remains balanced because everyone involved gains. It may also not lean because the exchange is weightless, meaningless.

The number 6: Past, present and future, penetration
Symbols: Libra, brown headgear
Detail: The four small coins

The challenge: In order to be able to give correctly, we must be able to receive correctly. Those who are unable to receive will have a hard time even learning what assistance means. What is called for is active support, work and promotion of talents or projects.

What you can do: Make sure you do not focus on scarcity but rather on achieving profit. If you use your talents to meet needs and inspire and promote talents based on your needs, true benefits will be achieved every time. Cooperation with others, when you are able to show weaknesses without provoking strength (and vice versa), produces a balanced give and take and a sense of community.

Mindfulness: Practice the Jnana mudra*: All fingers are outstretched, the index fingers are bent and their tips touch the tips of the thumbs. A circle is formed by this contact. The rest of the fingers remain extended but relaxed. The Jnana mudra stimulates the root chakra, calms and improves concentration, brightens your mood and gives inner peace.

STOCKTAKING
Observe, Wait, and See

Seven of Coins

Picture and message: A new coin is added to the six already there, or it is contrasted with them. This coin is at the feet of the figure in the picture. It makes a difference whether you look at a situation or project primarily out of habit and routine or whether you are open to a fresh and alternative perspective.

The number 7: Seven days, years, wonders of the world
Symbols: Hoe, different-colored soil
Detail: Different-colored shoes

The challenge: What is important in this card is the personal view of the one who asks the question: What preoccupies him, and what would he like to do? Six coins indicate what exists, what has been. One coin grows next to them. The value of a new idea is not measured by what is but by what will be.

What you can do: Pause and take stock! And ask questions: This is about the value and sense of what you have achieved so far and about setting new goals. Which results and achievements have been worthwhile? Which ones haven't? Are you satisfied with your results? With how you did your work? Every situation tells a story. Certain clues and signs are worth studying and interpreting. This card is also about your personal significance, your standpoint and your attitude. Keep calm and watch your harvest grow, while you check whether you're going to do things differently in future or not.

Mindfulness: "The grass doesn't grow faster if you pull on it," says an African proverb.

LOVE FOR THE WORK
Uniting Heaven and Earth

Eight of Coins

Picture and message: The goldsmith stamps his work and his work stamps him. Meanwhile the coins with the pentagram, the five-pointed star, are a mirror for a human being. The card concerns specific results: work, and creating your own living environment, in which the smith can manifest and immortalize himself, his personality, his values.

The number 8: Upright infinity symbol, cyclical change
Symbols: Bench, apron, hammer, and chisel
Detail: The road to town

The challenge: To do what we love with care, love, patience and skill means to appreciate our talents and the work we are able to do thanks to these talents. All professional and household work is also a symbol for work on ourselves. Perhaps we need to learn new skills for this work; at any rate, it takes new commitment and focusing.

What you can do: See that you have rewarding experiences that bear your signature, your individual style, and in which you can recognize yourself. Thus, little by little, you will create a situation of healthy prosperity: Ideas that have been implemented and wishes that have been fulfilled are something wonderful. Engage with your tasks fully and create a living environment and goals that are completely your own.

Mindfulness: According to Gautama Buddha, "The carpenter works the wood. The marksman bends the bow. The wise man forms himself."

PRODUCE ABUNDANT FRUIT
No Man Is an Island

Nine of Coins

Picture and message: A person is staying in a fertile garden, the grapes are ripe, flowers ornament the robe, and the tamed falcon perches on a golden glove. Personal flowering is achieved when we feel the joy of being alive and when we are satisfied with our own talents. We need to enjoy what we are. And it is important to let things grow and prosper.

The number 9: Abundance, complexity
Symbols: Falcon, golden glove, vineyard
Detail: Snail

The challenge: It makes a big difference whether we are in the world or not. Each of us has something to contribute that makes the world richer. The grapes represent commitment, hard work and a good harvest. "Anyone who imagines that all fruits ripen at the same time as the strawberries knows nothing about grapes," says Paracelsus.

What you can do: Be generous and respectfully show your fellow humans what treasures you have to offer because you yourself are a treasure. Depending on your view the figure in the picture is standing in front of or behind the hedge. Distancing is good, but you shouldn't hide your talents. The little snail in the picture teaches you the art of always being at home with yourself. Try to decode additional details of the picture to further interpret this card.

Mindfulness: "It is not the fortunate who are grateful. It is the grateful who are fortunate," says Francis Bacon. Be grateful to life, be grateful to yourself for what you make possible.

ABUNDANT LIFE
Magical Moments

Ten of Coins

Picture and message: Ten coins are the ten stations of the tree of life in the Kabbala. Behind them, life is revealed in all its abundance. An old man at the end of his life's journey watches the scene knowingly. A man and woman face each other in conversation, the child clings to the mother's skirt. The dogs have been guarding the gate, the sky is bright blue.

The number 10: High point, conclusion and reorientation
Symbols: Family, animals, castle gate
Detail: Grapes on the wise man's cloak

The challenge: We are all part of the great cycles of life. Each of us experiences the world from many perspectives, stages and circumstances. Nothing and no one is separate from family, ancestors, nature and the universe. We should consciously realize how our own actions are based on those of the ancients, continuing and passing them on.

What you can do: Truly open your eyes and see the abundance of the world around you. Take pleasure in it and enjoy your world and yourself in the middle of it. Experience what it feels like to have arrived in the here and now. The ten coins are a mirror of the gift you've been given and of your achievements, your inherited talents and the values you've created. They will tell your story even long after you have passed away.

Mindfulness: Be aware of your share in world events. Experience yourself as part of creation and of the cosmic flow. What is unique and individual about you is thus transformed from a transitory individual case to a conscious and enduring part of history.

Mindful of New Horizons

"One road to reality is by way of pictures." *

Mindfulness is attentive observation characterized by nonjudgmental openness and unbiased investigation of that which is observed. Such observation may refer to anything—anything that is happening in us and around us, including our own feelings and needs.

A particularly good opportunity to practice mindful awareness and to refresh it again and again is an encounter with pictures. During his years of study in Vienna, Elias Canetti, the graduate chemist and recipient of a Nobel Prize in Literature, had lasting experiences with works of visual art. His experiences perfectly express what we may experience when mindfully contemplating any kind of picture, and thus also what the mindful contemplation of tarot pictures has to offer us.

"One road to reality is by way of pictures," realized Elias Canetti and added, "I don't believe there's any better road. You adhere to something that doesn't change, thus exhausting the ever changing. Pictures are nets, and what appears in them is the holdable catch. Some things slip through the meshes and some go rotten, but you keep on trying, you carry the nets around with you, cast them out and they grow stronger from their catches.

"However, it's important that these pictures exist outside a person, too; inside a human being, even they are subject to change. There has to be a place where he can find them intact, not he alone, a place where everyone who feels uncertain can find them. Whenever a man feels the precariousness of his experience, he turns to a picture. Here, experience holds still, he can look into its face. He thus calms down by knowing reality, which is his own, although merely depicted here.

"Apparently it would be there even without him, but these appearances are deceiving; the pictures need his experience in order to awake. That is why pictures slumber for generations: no one can see them with the experience that awakes them."

Pictures Are Doors

The way Canetti describes his experiences with the pictures at the museum also provides amazing information for our understanding of mindful tarot practice today:

- **"Pictures are nets":** Here Canetti addresses the fact that pictures (when they speak to us in some way) make visible feelings, moods and motives in the deeper layers of our personality.
- **What do these "nets" catch?** Their catch is our inner sensations and concerns. It is not only dreams at night that go fishing in the ocean of the unconscious, so to speak. Pictures, films and other things can do this as well.
- **Background:** We perceive what we see in a holistic way. Like a movement we're observing, a picture that speaks to us also constantly triggers intuitive reactions and inner emotions in us.
- **"There has to be a place where he can find them [the pictures] intact":** Compared to other meditation techniques that work purely with ideas and images of the inner world (with dreams, visions, imaginary journeys, etc.), one important difference here is that the pictures exist in the outside world and that there is a place where these pictures are available unchanged.
- **"Here, experience holds still, he can look into its face":** If we repeatedly confront the same pictures, with which we are actually already familiar, then as time goes by we can observe how our perspective in perceiving the same picture varies and evolves. That is a most rewarding, exciting and at the same time relaxing experience. Moreover, it is how we get to know the *power of projection*.

- **"Knowing reality":** On different days, as moods change or during different phases of life, the same picture can have a totally differently effect on us and even look different to us. Something similar happens to us in daily life as well, though we are unaware of it; we easily identify with impressions received on a particular day.

The mindful contemplation of a picture is good training for us: We learn to notice our projections more easily and to become more sensitive to them in our daily lives as well.

- **"The pictures need [our] experience in order to awake":** We realize how much we ourselves put into our perception of a situation. Every perception also contains a bit of our personal contribution to perception, in which we ourselves play an active role.
- **"Whenever he [the person] feels the precariousness of his experience, he turns to a picture":** Here Canetti is referring to the fact that pictures can give us support and comfort us. They have something to tell us. They do not judge our situation; they throw light on it.

When pictures make an impression on us, they function like doors and portals. They lead to a deeper personal reality.

Because pictures invite the viewer to attentive contemplation and because over time they open up ever new perspectives, they are particularly suitable in training for mindful living and as an accompaniment to a mindful life. This is what Elias Canetti suggests when he says, "One road to reality is by way of pictures."

Arthur E. Waite, too, was obviously thinking along the same lines when, together with Pamela Colman Smith, he developed his new tarot, which for the first time in history showed scenes on all the tarot cards. In the book that accompanied his cards he noted:

"The pictures are like doors which open into unexpected chambers, or like a turn in the open road with a wide prospect beyond." *

Symbolic Languages:
Keys to Deeper Understanding

The true tarot is symbolism,
it speaks no other language
*and offers no other signs. ***
—ARTHUR E. WAITE

When interpreting tarot pictures,* it's worth looking for parallels in related symbolic languages. Such motifs as the dove, serpent and wolf, for instance, specific characters, elements, colors and many others have the same meanings in tarot, in astrology, in fairy tales and myths as well as in the interpretation of dreams.

Water, for example, represents the soul, spiritual life in all its facets.

- Whether you dream at night of a shower or a swimming pool,
- whether you are fascinated by a fairy tale about a fountain of youth,
- whether you are fascinated by myths that tell of the water of life,
- whether you have a special history with the zodiac signs Cancer, Scorpio and Pisces, or
- whether tarot cards with cups or bodies of water particularly affect you—in every instance a similar theme relating to our inner life may be involved.

The meanings of a symbol are multilayered, but always concentrate on specific thematic fields. These symbolic meanings are basically identical, regardless of whether we're dealing with fairy tales, myths, dreams, tarot or astrology or with tarot, Lenormand, Kipper or other pictorial cards. (Only simple playing cards like poker and skat cards belong to another category, because they have no picture motifs.)

Tarot and Astrology

Astrology had its origin several thousand years ago. Tarot cards, on the other hand, are considerably more recent, though they too date back almost six hundred years. Links between the symbol systems of tarot and astrology were not established until the end of the nineteenthcentury.

The most popular tarot deck was the "Golden Dawn"* combination, shown on the following double page. In the Waite tarot deck the astrological signs the cards are associated with sometimes appear directly in the picture of the card (e.g., the Aries sign in card no. IV–The Emperor—or the Taurus sign in the King of Coins picture).

The link between tarot and astrology is a bonus, not a must for tarot interpretation. In the following table, if you are interested, you will find sets of six tarot cards each that are associated with a sign of the zodiac.

The arm rests of the Emperor's throne are adorned with the sign for Aries.

Which zodiac sign are you most interested in right now? Take the corresponding six cards from your tarot game and look at them carefully, meditating on them from time to time. All six together form an image for the meaning of the respective zodiac sign.

The six cards of a zodiac sign mostly embody a certain tension pattern, which is important for understanding the respective zodiac sign.

The example of Aries: Here, within the set of six cards there is the contrast between Emperor and Tower, between buildup and decline of power; there is also the contrast between Emperor and Queen of Wands, between male and female fire energy, the connection between which is shown among other things in the picture of the card for Four of Wands.

The example of Scorpio: Death and rebirth, the principle "Die and become!" as represented by the cards for Death and Judgement.

Steer heads (for Taurus) ornament the throne of the King of Coins.

Date	Zodiac	Planet	MAJOR CARD of the ZODIAC
21.3.–20.4.	Aries	Mars	IV – The Emperor
21.4.–21.5.	Taurus	Venus	V – The Hierophant
22.5.–21.6.	Gemini	Mercury	VI – The Lovers
22.6.–22.7.	Cancer	Moon	VII – The Chariot
23.7.–22.8.	Leo	Sun	VIII – Strength
23.8.–22.9.	Virgo	Mercury	IX – The Hermit
23.9.–22.10.	Libra	Venus	XI – Justice
23.10.–21.11.	Scorpio	Pluto	XIII – Death
22.11.–21.12.	Sagittarius	Jupiter	XIV – Temperance
22.12.–20.1.	Capricorn	Saturn	XV – The Devil
21.1.–19.2.	Aquarius	Uranus	XVII – The Star
20.2.–20.3.	Pisces	Neptune	XVIII – The Moon

corresponding FACE CARD	corresponding PIP CARDS	MAJOR CARD of the PLANET
Wand Queen	Wand 2–4	XVI–The Tower
Coin King	Coin 5–7	III–The Empress
Sword Knight	Sword 8–10	I–The Magician
Cup Queen	Cup 2–4	II–The High Priestess
Wand King	Wand 5–7	XIX–The Sun
Coin Knight	Coin 8–10	I–The Magician
Sword Queen	Sword 2–4	III–The Empress
Cup King	Cup 5–7	XX–Judgement
Wand Knight	Wand 8–10	X–Wheel of Fortune
Coin Queen	Coin 2–4	XXI–The World
Sword King	Sword 5–7	XXII/0–The Fool
Cup Knight	Cup 8–10	XII–The Hanged Man

QUEEN of CUPS.

Appendix

Notes

P. 1 Definition of mindfulness: Here is a small selection of the numerous books. Halko Weiss, Michael E. Harrer, and Thomas Dietz: *The Mindfulness Book*, Stuttgart 2015, 2019 (see also www.achtsamleben.at). **Jon** Kabat-Zinn: *Mindfulness for Beginners,* Freiburg 2013; same author: *Healthy through Meditation: The Great Book of Self-Healing with MBSR,* Munich 2011, 2013. Thích Nhất Hạnh: *The Miracle of Mindfulness,* Stuttgart, 2002. As well as three lectures from Jean Gebser: *On Playing Success*, *On the Value of Obstacles*, and *On Experience*, Audio CD and audiobook, Novalis, 2000 (also print editions).

P. 2 "Chance favors the prepared mind:" Original French: *Le hasard [, d'ailleurs,] favorise les esprits préparés [...],"* by Pasteur Vallery-Radot (ed.): Œuvres de Pasteur. *Volume 6: Maladies virulentes, virus-vaccins et prophylaxie de la rage.* Paris: Masson, 1933, 348.

P. 2 Coincidence as a meaningful part of reality: Stefan Klein, *Everything Coincidence: The Power that Determines our Life.* Reinbek, 2004. Jacques Monod, *Chance and Necessity: Philosophical Questions in Modern Biology.* Munich, 1971. As well as the German Physical Society (DPG), *Discovery of Chance: 100 Years of Quantum Theory.* Bad Honnef, 2000.

P. 2 Serendipity: Cf. Miriam Meckel/Daniel Rettig, *Serendipity: 77 Accidental Discoveries That Made History,* Zurich, 2018; as well as English-language serendity titles by Umberto Eco and Thomas K. Merton.

P. 6 Predictive Coding: Jordana Cepelewicz, *Predictive Coding: Does Our Brain Predict the Future?* in *Spektrum*, April 22, 2019, https: //www.spektrum. de/news/our-brains-predicts-the-future/1613666; and Bruce E. Goldstein, *Perceptual Psychology*, Heidelberg, 2002; as well as (of general importance, not only for musicians) Robert Jourdain, *The Well-Tempered Brain: How Music Arises and Works in the Head*, Heidelberg, 2001.

P. 7 "Talent for Fate": Novalis (actually Georg Philipp Friedrich von Hardenberg): "Luck Is Talent for History, or for Fate"; in: The same, *The General Brouillon. Materials for Encyclopedia* 1798/9; quoted from https://famous-zitate.de/zitate/124028-novalis-gluck-ist-talent-fur-die-historie-oder-das-schick.

P. 36 and 105 "Mudra": More about mudras in Gertrud Hirschi, *Mudras for Body, Mind and Soul*, Krummwisch, 2009.

P. 111 "The way to reality … through pictures": Elias Canetti, *The Torch in the Ear*, Munich, Vienna, 1980, 130; Paperback edition Frankfurt, M. 1982, 109.

P. 113 "An image that speaks to us triggers … inner movements in us": Among other things, these are effective here, the mechanisms of *Identification, Ideomotor Skills (aka Carpenter effect) and Intuition.*

113 "The pictures are like doors": Arthur E. Waite, *The Pictorial Key to the Tarot.* London, 1910, 169, translation into German by the author. The term *doors* has a special tradition in English. William Blake coined the famous saying around 1790, "There are things known, and things unknown, and in-between are [the] doors," and, "There are known things and unknown things, and there are doors in between." This saying later to achieved a far-reaching meaning through Aldous Huxley, the rock group The Doors, the *Harry Potter* series and many others. Arthur E. Waite was a forerunner, a spiritual pioneer, when he developed the modern reissue of the traditional tarot in 1909/1910. Waite's autobiography (A. E. Waite, *Shadows of Life and Thought*, 1938) and the excellent biography by R. A. Gilbert, *AE Waite. Magician of Many Parts,* Wellingborough, UK 1987, German edition R. A. Gilbert, *Arthur E. Waite. A Magician of a Special Kind,* Krummwisch, 1998.

P. 114 "Tarot is symbolism …": Arthur E. Waite, *The Pictorial Key to the Tarot.* 1910; quoted here from the German edition: Arthur E. Waite, *Der Bilderschüssel zum Tarot,* Waakirchen, 1978, 33.

P.114 Cross-connections/same meanings in different symbolic languages:

a) Cf. classics of psychological symbol interpretation, among others. C. G. Jung, The Human Being and his Symbols; the same: Symbols and Dream Interpretation (anthology); Erich Fromm: Fairy Tales, Myths, Dreams. An Introduction to Understanding a Forgotten Language; Works by Hans Dieckmann and Marie-Louise von Franz. Many of these titles are available in numerous editions.—Marion Guekos-Holleinstein: Sources of the Tarot (Depth psychological interpretations and sources of cultural history.) Krummwisch 2000. This is a good representation.

b) Cf. current interpretation books that contain such cross-connections: **Johannes Fiebig/Evelin Bürger,** *Tarot: Ways of happiness.* Krummwisch 1993; same: Tarot Basics Waite. Krummwisch 2008; **Harald Jösten,** *Lenormand. Discover the Power in You!* Krummwisch 2017, 2018; **Pia Schneider/Stella Bernheim,** *Kipper Cards for Beginners.* Krummwisch 2018; **Susanne Peymann,** *The Pendulum Box for Beginners.* Krummwisch 2016; **Klausbernd Vollmar,** *Interpretation of Dreams. Everything You need to Know.* Krummwisch 2011; **Klausbernd Vollmar/ Johannes Fiebig,** *Dream and Dream Interpretation - Experience and Understand.* Krummwisch 1999; **Johannes Fiebig/Eva-Christiane Wetterer,** *Magical Companion Pocket Calendar.* 2012–2024. Krummwisch 2011; **Ernst Ott:** *Astrology with Tarot.* Tübingen 2005; Klausbernd **Vollmar:** *The Great Book of Colors.* 5th edition. Krummwisch 2017.

P. 115 Golden Dawn: Find out more about this important English Rosicrucian order: **Israel Regardie (ed.),** *The Magical System of the Golden Dawn.* 3 volumes. Freiburg 1998; as well as the unique standard work on esoteric tarot in the 19th century: **Eckard Graf,** *The Magicians of the Tarot.* Krummwisch 2000.

Bibliograpy

Fiebig, Johannes, and Evelin Bürger: *Tarot Basics Waite.* Krummwisch, Germany: Königsfurt-Urania, 2008. English edition under the title *The Ultimate Guide to the Rider Waite Tarot.* Woodbury, MN: Llewellyn Publications, 2013.

————. *The Great Book of Tarot Spreads.* Krummwisch, Germany: Königsfurt-Urania, 1995.

————. *Tarot for Beginners.* Munich: Heyne-Taschen Books, 2019.

————. *Tarot: Ways of Happiness.* Krummwisch, Germany: Königsfurt-Urania, 1993.

Fiebig, Johannes: *Dalí Tarot.* Taschen Verlag: Cologne, 2019.

————. *You Are What You Forget: The Test.* With illustrations by Urban Trösch. Krummwisch, Germany: Königsfurt-Urania, 2018.

Guekos-Holleinstein, Marion: *Sources of the Tarot.* Krummwisch, Germany: Königsfurt-Urania, 2000.

Haindl, Erika, Antje Betken, Johannes Fiebig (ed.): *Hermann Haindl: Life—Art—Tarot.* Krummwisch, Germany: Königsfirt-Urania, 2017.

Pollack, Rachel: *Tarot Wisdom: Spiritual Teachings and Practical Knowledge.* Krummwisch, Germany: Königsfirt-Urania, 2009.

Schwarz, Lilo: *The Great Tarot Practice Book.* Krummwisch, Germany: Königsfirt-Urania, 2018.

Wetterer, Eva-Christiane, and **Anja-Dorothee Schacht:** *Sentenzia. Fireheart & Wing Sword.* Krummwisch, Germany: Königsfirt-Urania, 2010.

To Write to the Authors

If you wish to contact the authors or would like more information about this book, please write to the authors in care of Llewellyn Worldwide Ltd. and we will forward your request. Both the authors and publisher appreciate hearing from you and learning of your enjoyment of this book and how it has helped you. Llewellyn Worldwide Ltd. cannot guarantee that every letter written to the authors can be answered, but all will be forwarded. Please write to:

Johannes Fiebig and Evelin Burger
℅ Llewellyn Worldwide
2143 Wooddale Drive
Woodbury, MN 55125-2989
Please enclose a self-addressed stamped envelope for reply,
or $1.00 to cover costs. If outside the U.S.A., enclose
an international postal reply coupon.

Many of Llewellyn's authors have websites with additional
information and resources. For more information,
please visit our website at http://www.llewellyn.com